MW01194798

THE ANGER RESET

27

DAYS TO A CALMER YOU

GIL STIEGLITZ

Spiritual Warfare Series

Book 1

PTLB

PRINCIPLES
TO LIVE BY

LIFE IS RELATIONSHIPS

The Anger Reset: 27 Days to a Calmer You

Book 1 of the Spiritual Warfare Series

Copyright © 2025 Gil Stieglitz

Published by PTLB Publishing, P.O. Box 214, Roseville, CA, 95661. For more information about this book and the author, visit www.ptlb.com.

ISBN: 978-1-952736-04-9 (paperback)
         978-1-952736-05-6 (e-book)

Copyediting and production by Jennifer Edwards, jedwardsediting.net

Cover design by Dave Eaton

Interior design by Ben Holman

Author photo credit: Hannah White

Cover photo credit: Craig Adderley

Interior photo credits: Leroy Skalstad (opposite pg 1), Andrea Piacquadio (pgs 14, 40 and 110), Tima Miroshnichenko (pg 24), Craig Adderley (pg 50), Kevin Bidwell (pg 58), Danya Gutan (pg 66), Jörge LINaan-Studio (pg 86), Totoosart Photography (pg 94), Engin Akyurt (pgs 102 and 156), Ekaterina Belinskaya (pg 118), Leroy Skalstad (pg 124), Praveen Kumar (pg 130), Vitaly Gorbachev (pg 148), Jean Marc Bonnel (pg 172).

All rights reserved. No part of this publication may be reproduced, stored in a retrieval system, or transmitted in any way by any means—electronic, mechanical, photocopy, recording, or otherwise—without the prior permission of the copyright holder, except as provided by USA copyright law. When reproducing text from this book, include the following credit line: *"The Anger Reset: 27 Days to a Calmer You* by Gil Stieglitz, published by PTLB Publishing. Used with permission."

Scripture quotations marked NASB come from the *NEW AMERICAN STANDARD BIBLE®*, Copyright © 1960, 1962, 1963, 1968, 1971, 1972, 1973, 1975, 1977, 1995 by The Lockman Foundation. Used by permission.

Scripture quotations marked NIV come from the *Holy Bible, New International Version®*, NIV® Copyright © 1973, 1978, 1984, 2011 by Biblica, Inc. ® Used by permission. All rights reserved worldwide.

Scripture quotations marked KJV come from the *Holy Bible, King James Version.*

Scripture quotations marked PHILLIPS come from the *J.B. Phillips New Testament. The New Testament in Modern English* by J.B. Phillips copyright © 1960, 1972 J. B. Phillips. Administered by The Archbishops' Council of the Church of England. Used by Permission.

Disclaimer: The information provided within this book is for general informational purposes only. While the author has attempted to provide up-to-date and correct information as of the date of this printing, there are no representations or warranties, express or implied, about the completeness, accuracy, reliability, suitability, or availability with respect to the information, products, services, or related graphics contained in this book for any purpose. Any use of the methods described within this book is the author's personal thoughts. They are not intended to be a definitive set of instructions for this project. You may discover other methods and materials to accomplish the same result.

Library of Congress Number: 2025905846

PRINTED IN THE UNITED STATES OF AMERICA

DEDICATION

To the men at Folsom Prison who have learned to overcome their angry pasts and live calmly and peacefully in a broken world.

CONTENTS

MY ANGER RESET JOURNEY

Hello, my name is Dr. Gil Stieglitz, and I am an anger-aholic.

Every day, anger presents itself as a solution to all kinds of problems. I have to fight to keep my emotions of anger, irritation, frustration, and rage from leaking out and laying waste to my relationships, work, and joy. Though I grew up in a typical middle-class family with two loving parents, I was an angry child for some reason. I don't remember a day growing up without punching something or someone. I hope there were some days without anger, but I don't really remember them.

In my late teens, I started to notice that my anger and rage were disrupting and destroying my relationships. You would think I would have noticed the damage before that, but I didn't. After I became a Christian, I knew that Christ wanted me to get a handle on my anger, so I set out to learn how to reset the level of anger in my life. Since then, I have discovered twenty-seven strategies that have worked for me. Some will work for you, and some probably won't, and that's okay! This book aims to help you find some strategies to reset and manage your anger instead of the other way around. For many people, anger rises up within them, and they have no way to stop it from forcing its way to the surface, demanding to be noticed. I want to help you build a calm life where your anger is not in charge, and God guides you in understanding, managing, and refining your rage so you can build a different kind of life.

Recently, I had the privilege of presenting a series of workshops using these twenty-seven strategies to a group of men serving time in Folsom Prison in California. They wanted to move beyond anger and knew they needed to control their anger if life was ever to get better for them. Many of these men had significant issues with anger, as you might imagine, so for three months, we worked through Scriptures, practiced anger-resetting workouts, and talked about what worked and what didn't. Today, many of these men are making progress in controlling this spiritual and emotional side of their lives.

You might have noticed I just used the word "spiritual" in relation to anger. I want everyone reading this book to realize that anger really is a form of spiritual warfare. It can either take hold of you and destroy you, or you can learn to control it by lowering its intensity and triggers. These men at the prison had taken lots of courses on anger management, but this was the first one that taught them what the Scriptures say about anger and provided biblical workouts to draw God's power into their battle with it.

In my personal journey with anger, the first step of my reset process took place when I admitted I couldn't control this emotion and its power on my own. As long as I thought I could handle it myself, I lost control regularly. I needed God to come into me in a new and direct way to guide, energize, and, at times, stop me from destroying the life I wanted. I wrote this book to show people with anger issues how to stay away from the dirty energy of anger. So, if you still believe you can handle this problem on your own, then this book may not be for you.

When I gave my life to Jesus Christ and asked Him to change me, control me, and develop me, that is when true healing began. God came in and immediately changed me—I saw it, and others saw it, too. He has also continued an ongoing developmental process to separate me from my anger. Thank God He did because I was headed for a very different life than I have now.

Before I became a Christian, back in my teen years, I was known as a hothead and very volatile. I regularly punched, raged, and yelled at people to get my way. However, something changed when I truly surrendered to Jesus Christ and asked Him to work with me on this anger problem. Proof of this change occurred shortly after my conversion to Christianity when my friends and I were playing basketball in the gym at school. I ran down to lead a fast break, yelling for the ball to be thrown to me. One of the guys on my team saw me and chucked the ball as hard as he could. The other team was coming fast, and I spread my hands a little too wide to receive the ball. Needless to say, it slammed into my face. It was going fast enough to break my glasses against my face, and all the glass shattered and fell to the floor. Those who knew me began backing up as they expected me to punch someone, knowing I would be angry. But instead of yelling, I heard myself say, "Be careful; don't anyone step in the glass. I'm okay." Everyone was amazed, including me! Something was different. Jesus was there working, changing me so I could think of others, not just myself and my pain.

I hope you consider asking Jesus Christ into your life as your Savior and Lord. In this spiritual battle with anger, you will need His wisdom, energy, love, and ideas to begin a new process of resetting your anger. I can't think of any other way to overcome anger than by starting a partnership with Jesus. Nothing else works for the long haul, believe me. Jesus has made all the difference in my life. If you want Him to intercede on your behalf and help you overcome your anger problem, you can ask Him to do so right now. Here is the prayer I prayed, and I invite you to pray it too:

Dear Heavenly Father,

I admit that I need you. I am a sinner and angry. I cannot control my anger on my own. I ask you to forgive me of my sins and become the boss of my life. Please make me the kind of person you want me to be. Thank you for dying on the cross to forgive me. I accept you as my Savior and my Lord.

In the Name of the Lord Jesus Christ, Amen

When you pray this sincere prayer of surrender to Jesus Christ and admit that you need His help, energy, and correction, it unleashes the God of Heaven's power. He hears you, and now He will take action. Overcoming anger on your own will not work long-term, but surrendering to Jesus Christ builds a whole different response when things don't go your way. It will work. I know because I have experienced it, and so have many others. Will you be perfectly calm after you pray this prayer? Not necessarily, but the process of resetting your anger will have begun.

"THE KEY TO AN ANGER RESET LIES IN PARTNERING WITH GOD, UNDERSTANDING IT, AND APPLYING THE WISDOM OF SCRIPTURE."

—Gil Stieglitz

DAY

WHAT SCRIPTURE SAYS ABOUT ANGER

Ephesians 4:25-32

You may not realize it, but managing the level of your anger is a command from God. He knows that uncontrolled anger has the propensity to ruin our lives, so He warns us and teaches us how to control it. The key to an anger reset lies in partnering with Him, understanding it, and applying the wisdom of Scripture. One passage that has profoundly impacted my life is Ephesians 4:25-32 (NIV). I have spent many years studying, reciting, and applying this powerful passage. I strongly suggest that you memorize these verses and meditate on their truths and spiritual power. There are numerous anger management strategies in this passage alone. Let's take a look.

> 25 Therefore each of you must put off falsehood and speak truthfully to your neighbor, for we are all members of one body.

> 26 "In your anger do not sin": Do not let the sun go down while you are still angry,

> 27 and do not give the devil a foothold.

[28] Anyone who has been stealing must steal no longer, but must work, doing something useful with their own hands, that they may have something to share with those in need.

[29] Do not let any unwholesome talk come out of your mouths, but only what is helpful for building others up according to their needs, that it may benefit those who listen.

[30] And do not grieve the Holy Spirit of God, with whom you were sealed for the day of redemption.

[31] Get rid of all bitterness, rage and anger, brawling and slander, along with every form of malice.

[32] Be kind and compassionate to one another, forgiving each other, just as in Christ God forgave you.

You can see this passage serves as both a caution and a guide. It acknowledges that anger is a natural emotion but warns against allowing it to lead to your life. It also emphasizes the importance of dealing with anger promptly and appropriately lest it festers and creates real damage. As you study and meditate on this passage, you may find other insights, but here here are eleven truths that jump out at me: truths that jumped out at me:

1. **Speak truth but not from anger (v. 25).** So often, we want to tell the truth from a place of anger instead of a place of benefit and wisdom. Resist telling your truth when you are angry. (I have gotten into trouble telling people my truth from a place of anger.)

2. **Feel your emotion but understand what your anger is trying to do (v. 26).** Many of us deny that we are angry. You can't fix what you are unwilling to admit is going on. Tell yourself and others that you are angry when you are angry. We seem foolish and petty when we say, "Oh, I am not angry!" when we clearly are angry. You can say, "I am flooded right now, and I need to calm down," or, "I am frustrated and reacting strongly to this situation."

3. **But do not sin—don't let it escape (v. 26)!** It is not a sin to feel angry. It becomes a sin when we use it to damage others and the situation. It is not sinful to feel frustrated, angry, upset, irritated, and the like—that is normal. It becomes a sin when you spew it out on others to get your way.

4. **Deal with your anger—don't let it fester (v. 26).** We all need systems to calm us down and deal with anger. You can't pretend it didn't happen—that's not a wise system. I usually laugh now when I see a person who is angry trying to pretend they are not angry. I understand what they are going through, but they need to deal with their anger and not stuff it down or deny it.

5. **Don't let your anger turn into a demonic attachment (v. 27).** If we give into anger to get our way, then we invite more and more spiritual battles into our lives. Using the power of anger to get what you want invites the devil to help you stay angry. The devil wants to make you a prisoner to anger. If you always give in to expressing your feelings (anger, depression, anxiety, loneliness, bitterness), then you can become a prisoner to those feelings.

6. **Perform good works you can share with others (v. 28).** Anger is a powerful self-focused mechanism. One of the key antidotes to anger and other negative emotions is to do something positive for others. In this way, you will switch from a self-centered focus to a wisdom focus.

7. **Speak positive words that build others up instead of angry, destructive words that tear them down (v. 29).** When we are angry, our natural reaction is to tear others down to get what we want, but we need to do the opposite. We need to point out what others are doing right and what we positively want that will allow everyone to benefit.

8. **Listen to the Holy Spirit; don't grieve Him (v. 30).** God still speaks today. It is incredible that in our self-focus, God will speak about what to do if we listen. He speaks quietly, like

a whisper, when we are tempted to do something we know we shouldn't. You have to be willing to listen carefully for His whisper rather than just giving in to the emotion you are feeling.

9. **There are at least six forms anger usually takes—bitterness, wrath, anger, clamor, slander, and malice (v. 31).** Each of us has one or more typical paths of anger. Find the ones you usually use and prepare to do something else instead of giving in to your favorite destructive tendency.

10. **Substitute anger with kindness, tender-heartedness, and forgiveness (v. 32).** When you listen to God, He will direct you to a broader perspective—one full of kindness, tender-heartedness, and forgiveness. It is too easy to seek our own justice for our grievances, and God wants us to be bigger than that.

11. **Realize how much God, through Christ, has forgiven you (v. 32).** Jesus and the writers of the New Testament regularly bring up how much we have been forgiven. God wants us to remember that truth when tempted to extract our pound of flesh from the person who wronged us.

Resetting the level of your anger is possible and worthwhile. There are relationships, jobs, promotions, and opportunities that will grow in your life as you learn to be calm. People need to feel safe around you. I always appreciated when someone would share an insight that helped me cooperate with God on my journey to control and calmness. Now I am sharing what I have learned to help you. Please use these exercises and prayers to allow God to make you a safe person to be around.

FINDING MORE TRUTHS ABOUT ANGER
(EPHESIANS 4:25-32)

Throughout this book, we will walk through life-changing biblical techniques to reset your anger over twenty-seven days. Each comes with a spiritual workout to practice and incorporate the technique into your life. God wants to help you become the person He knows you can be, but it will require your cooperation with Him and doing what He says to do in His Word. It is not enough to call Him "Lord, Lord," you must also do what He says (Luke 6:46). This, then, begins the process of being set apart for God's purposes—a process Scripture calls sanctification. This is where your mind begins to be renewed and transformed to see God's perspective and wisdom (Romans 12:2).

For today's spiritual workout, I would like you to write Ephesians 4:25-32 in a notebook or use the Notes app on your phone. I have provided eleven different ways this passage talks about mastering your anger, but other truths must be gleaned. Go through this passage again, line by line, and pay attention to what God may be telling you. Is there anything else that sticks out to you? Do certain words or passages jump out at you? What do you sense God is telling you? Write whatever thoughts come to your mind and spend the rest of the day thinking about how they apply to your anger issues.

GAINING MASTERY OVER YOUR ANGER

Understanding the need for divine intervention is crucial, and it begins with prayer. Each day, I will include several prayers for you to pray for God's help in this journey to peace, calm, and control. Pray each prayer with sincerity and invite the Lord Jesus into your life at new levels. Even though God performed a huge miracle at the beginning of my Christian life, I still need His help each day to choose wisdom over foolishness.

Today, I recommend praying this prayer for strength to begin. It asks for God's help in controlling anger. Print or write it out and pray it at the beginning of each day while on this twenty-seven-day journey.

Dear Heavenly Father,

I admit I cannot control my anger on my own. I need You to be in me, with me, over me, and through me. Please come into my life at a new level today and save me from my own destructive reactions. Thank You for dying on the cross for my sins. I trust You to teach me new ways of thinking, acting, speaking, and being calm. I trust You, Lord Jesus, rather than my old ways.

In the Name of the Lord Jesus Christ, Amen

D A Y

2

ANGER IS RAW, DESTRUCTIVE ENERGY

Ephesians 4:26

Many people believe that anger is a superpower that allows them to get their way, just like the Incredible Hulk in the comics.[1] They have watched others go into rage mode to get what they want, but little do they know their rage will not lead to good relationships or a great life. The anger is too destructive when it is raw and unrefined. People used to give me Hulk t-shirts and called me the Hulk after I let my anger show in various situations. Sadly, it was not a compliment. I didn't like being thought of that way, so I needed to find a way to control my anger and not let it out.

All emotions are subjective reactions to the outside world. Happiness, sadness, anger, love, fear, or even hatred are caused by circumstances, moods, or the people in your life. Without emotions, life becomes a dull and lifeless place. We need emotions to accomplish critical actions, each one with its own kind of energy. Grief gives you the energy to be sad and reflective. Love gives you the energy to sacrifice, adapt, and give to others. Anger gives us the energy to bring about change, whether positive or negative.

Fear gives you the energy to fight or flee. When under control and refined, emotions produce a rich and enjoyable life, but if they are raw and unharnessed, they can overwhelm our lives and others.

The Bible says in Ephesians, "Be angry but do not sin" (Ephesians 4:26). God knows when our anger is raw, we usually want to change another person when we really need to change ourselves or our circumstances. **The goal is to use whatever energy an emotion produces without letting it dominate our lives** or dictate what we do. Knowing raw anger is almost always destructive, we need to learn to control, refine, redirect, and aim that energy at the right thing. How many times have you seen a boss or a spouse yelling because they want something to change? Letting anger spew onto other people will not make a positive difference. When have you responded positively to being yelled at? My guess is probably never.

If you've ever had a boss who used raw anger to try to get things done around the office, you've probably wondered, as an employee, how to get away from this destructive, demotivating tirade. Instead of being motivated to try harder, it's likely you were demotivated by the boss's destructive display of raw energy. Sure, some of your coworkers might have scurried around trying to appear busy, but usually in a way that was counterproductive to what the boss wanted. It would be so much more productive if the boss were able to contain his or her anger, refine it, and give the employees energy in the form of vision, permissions, money, hires, and so forth. Refine the anger and give them productive energy so they can use it to accomplish the changes needed.

This applies to parenting as well. Have you seen a parent unleashing an angry rant at their children? The children are scared but do not know what to do. They do not get more energy to do what their parent wants them to do when they are being yelled at. Instead, they want to get away from the angry parent or calm them down. Only if the parent can refine their raw anger into useable energy can the children act correctly.

Raw anger is a form of poor communication. Your angry non-verbals communicate so loudly that nobody can pay attention to the specific words you are using. We think that if we add emotion to our communication, what we mean will be more clear. But when anger is the emotion you add to your words, it muddies the message. The key is to calm down and communicate in a positive and energizing way.

IDENTIFY AND COMMUNICATE WHAT YOU WANT TO CHANGE IN A POSITIVE WAY

When you feel yourself getting angry, it is your body's way of saying, "I want something to change." The first question you have to answer before you let any of your anger out is, "What change do I want to see happen?" The second question you have to answer is, "How do I ask for the change in a positive and thoughtful way?" I have always been impressed with leaders who can hold their frustration and anger in while they begin to describe the positives that need to happen. They make positive requests calmly as they lead the group through an exercise in what could change a situation. You may be able to tell that they are agitated, but they are not spewing.

When it comes to positive changes for the people in our lives, we have to think carefully about what might cause them to change. It will rarely be to get angry at them, criticize or demean them, threaten them, or guilt them into changing. Anger wants instant action, but in its raw form, it is almost always negative. "I want you to stop doing that!" "I never want to see that happen again!" "Stop being so lazy." "I can't handle you asking me to do more!" "This is your job, start doing it." "Why don't you just do what I say?!" Effective change will often require lots of thought and lots of planning. Until you can verbalize the changes you want in a positive and thoughtful request, you are not ready to say anything. Yes, you can try to force people to change by spewing anger, but it is not helpful in the long run.

Raw anger lives in a fantasy land where everything should happen instantaneously, but real change requires wisdom, planning, and constructive ideas. You may find it helpful to carry a card with the following prompts on it or have it on your phone to help you think when anger is rising.

1. What is the change I want to happen?

2. What are all the things that could change in this situation?

   - The planning
   - Them (certain people)
   - Me (in some way)
   - The situation
   - The amount of time
   - The tone of voice
   - The level of noise or conversation

3. How can I change to bring peace and calm to this situation?

4. What could I change in the future so I would not be so angry about this?

5. How could these changes be made?

6. When could these changes happen?

The Bible is clear—anger becomes sin when we express it in its raw form: "Be angry but do not sin" (Ephesians 4:26). Are you able to contain your anger until wisdom catches up with your emotions? I am not talking about stuffing anger but rather processing it and refining it. We must build mental systems to occupy our emotions until God's wisdom can refine or redirect our anger. As you feel yourself getting angry, tell yourself, "There are other perspectives about this situation that I can't even imagine right now; I need to wait until I can hear them." Spewing your anger on those close to you before understanding all the facts can damage and even destroy a relationship.

We all want peace and great relationships. We think that anger is the magic shortcut that will get us what we want, but it won't. I have watched so many marriages, families, friendships, and businesses destroyed because of raw, unprocessed anger. Anger twists and distorts reality, and anger dominates relationships. Yes, we were wronged. Yes, we suffered injustice. Yes, we suffered a great loss. But if we do not learn how to control our reactions, the raw anger will lay waste to relationships and peace. Raw anger needs to be controlled, refined, used, and directed to positive means, and it can be with God's guidance. Your anger can help you accomplish a lot, but only if you refine it.

Also, just because you have an emotion doesn't mean that it needs to be expressed. Being angry and not sinning is like revving the engine of a car but not popping the clutch. It can be like flexing a muscle but not lifting anything. Just because you feel anger doesn't mean any other people need to know about it. Anger doesn't have to be in charge. Yes, you can temporarily get your way through rage and anger, but you won't get what you really want in the end.

CALM-DOWN CARD: RESET YOUR ANGER

Create a calm-down card by taking a 3" x 5" index card and writing James 1:19 on the front side. On the back, write a list of actions like the ones below to do whenever you start feeling angry. Pull out this card whenever you feel anger rising within you. Read the card. Lower your shoulders. Take a deep breath in and out. Repeat James 1:19 five different times:

> "Let everyone be quick to hear, slow to speak and slow to anger."
> **(James 1:19)**

Look at this list every time you feel anger rising. Then, do whatever is on this list that will increase your peace and calm.

- ❑ Admit to yourself, "I am feeling angry."
- ❑ How do I keep from letting this anger out?
- ❑ Pray and confess: "I am feeling angry right now."
- ❑ Step away from the situation.
- ❑ Don't say or do anything.
- ❑ Calm and relax your body.
- ❑ Realize you are being flooded right now.
- ❑ Say, "I am flooded right now, and I need a moment."
- ❑ Quote Scripture in your mind (Eph. 4:26; James 1:19).
- ❑ Change what you are thinking about.
- ❑ Think about something positive.
- ❑ Go do a workout or take a walk.
- ❑ Listen rather than respond: "That is interesting … tell me more."
- ❑ Count to 100.
- ❑ Get a different perspective.

CHANGING RAW ANGER INTO USABLE ENERGY

This prayer will help you prevent anger from overwhelming your life and destroying relationships. Put it on your phone or print it out and keep it in your pocket. Have it available to pray multiple times each day until you have developed some of these systems and strategies.

Dear Heavenly Father,

I have all this raw energy to bring about change, but I need to know how to stay calm. I don't know how to change it into usable energy. Show me, Lord, how to change my anger so it is useable and positive. Lord, you have given me all this energy to make something of myself and positively impact the world. Show me how to do that. Show me how to stay calm on the outside with all of this energy on the inside.

In Jesus Christ's Name, Amen

"WE CAN CREATE A GAP BETWEEN THE STIMULUS OF OUR ANGER AND OUR RESPONSE TO CHOOSE GOOD, BETTER, OR BEST."

—Gil Stieglitz

D A Y

3

INSTALL AN ANGER REFINERY

Proverbs 14:29

I was at a conference recently, explaining how anger often rises within me and how I have to slow it down. I have spent years putting systems in place to not let my anger reach a boiling point where it spills out on those around me. A very nicely dressed businessman approached me after the session and said, "Yes, that is what anger does inside me! It rises up, and I don't know what to do or how to control it. It just explodes onto others like a sneeze or cough. I need to fix this." As an anger-aholic, I totally understood. This man needed to build a refinery to slow down his anger.

The purpose of any refinery is to take a substance in its raw or natural state and make it pure and useful, such as oil or sugar. Anger is a raw emotion; in its natural or raw state, it's no good to us. I would even say it's harmful to you and those around you. But you can refine the useful energy from your anger by slowing the anger way down. I read in a book by Viktor Frankl, a survivor of the Auschwitz concentration camp in World War II, that it is possible to create a gap between the stimulus of your anger and your response.[2] It is in this gap that you gain the ability to choose what is good, better, and best. Too often we have been stimulated by anger and immediately respond as our anger wants us to. That is why we have to work on this process of refining our anger.

Many of us have successfully gotten people to do what we want through ANGER, so we do more of it. If you do this now or have done so in the past, notice if your anger has destroyed any of your relationships. This pattern of letting anger out onto others starts very young. It may have become habitual, but we must find ways to break this pattern and become calm. The Bible talks of this in Proverbs 14:29 (NASB, emphasis mine):

> "One who is **slow to anger** has great understanding; But one who is quick-tempered exalts foolishness."
> **(Proverbs 14:29)**

To overcome anger and refine its intensity, we must inject new skills and actions into our responses. Creating a gap is one thing we can do as this allows your anger to slow down, let wisdom catch up, and get your emotions out of the driver's seat. Another thing we can do is become better communicators since we know raw anger is a poor communicator.

PRACTICING BETTER COMMUNICATION SKILLS

When we are angry internally and externally, we become lousy communicators. Our heart rate races above 100 beats per minute and most rational thoughts are gone. We just want something to be different. We want something to stop NOW! We want whoever it is to listen to what we are saying. If we allow anger to rise and take control, we can expect negativity and emotional arrows to fly out of our mouths and bodies. We may try to say something good, but it will not be communicated in a way they will receive it. Relationships and lasting change require good communication. Going back and forth with real people with different perspectives is how to resolve conflicts and build connected relationships. Anger doesn't want connected relationships; it wants servants who will do what it wants.

We can learn to be better communicators by knowing what good communication is and practicing the skills we learn. Take a look at the top communication skills below. You and I need to be good at these skills, even when our emotions try to take them away. Practice these positive skills whenever you can. They don't come naturally, especially when we are filled with emotion. But the more you practice, the better you will communicate, even when part of you is filled with anger.

THE TOP COMMUNICATION SKILLS

ACTIVE LISTENING. Can you keep asking the other person questions about the situation even when you are full of anger? Practice on the people at work and home until you can focus on what the other person is saying, even if a lot is happening in your mind.

FRIENDLINESS. Most people are naturally self-focused and want to talk about their interests. Friendliness is really just thinking of the other person and talking about or doing what they want to at the moment. Anger makes us all hyper-self-focused on ourselves. We need to fight to stay open to other ideas, other points of view, and other people's interests. Remain friendly—this will be a rebuke to your anger.

CONFIDENCE. This is realizing that people want to talk about themselves and not what you probably want to discuss. Ask them questions about themselves and what they have found interesting in the last week or month. You can ask them about a topic you are interested in, but don't be surprised if that is not what they want to talk about for very long.

SHARING FEEDBACK. Make sure that you have listened before you offer feedback. Before you tell people what you think, ask, "Can I give you a different perspective?" If the other person is uninterested in your feedback, don't give it. Finding a way to offer controlled and positive feedback is a rebuke to your anger. Letting out your anger in its raw form is destructive feedback.

RECEIVING FEEDBACK. When someone gives you feedback, even if you don't want it or expect it, thank them and let them know that you will consider it. You can later evaluate if the feedback is sound or if the source is dubious. You can always discard it later, but thank them in the moment. Their feedback may trigger your anger. Build a system to receive, understand, evaluate, and discard people's feedback.

VOLUME AND CLARITY. Sometimes, we find ourselves unconsciously being loud, insistent, or aggressive because our anger energizes our conversation. Keep calm and speak slowly. Keep checking to see if you are going on a rant about something you care deeply about, but few others do. You'll see it on their faces.

EMPATHY. This means embracing the level of pain, hurt, or difficulty in other people's lives. We may be mad at people until we understand the stuff going on in their lives. Be willing to slow down and know what they are going through, even if you are going through a lot. Listen to them and feel their pain, and it will slow down your anger.

RESPECT. In what ways can you acknowledge another person's dignity and value? What are the positives about them? We may not appreciate what they just did, but they still have value as a person. Many people will only allow someone who respects them to help them improve. Be prepared to share ten positive actions or qualities about the people you are around regularly.

COURTEOUS RESPONSE. Our anger can cut off our responsiveness to others. This is why we have basic manners. "Please," "May I?" "Excuse me," and "Thank you" are ways to respond that slow down angry desires. We need to respond to others with a greeting, a question, or a courteous response of some kind.

All of the above are difficult to do when feeling angry, bitter, or unjustly treated. Practice these good communication skills. Realize our anger is a test that is trying to shut down good communication. Keep focusing on these positive ways to act and stay calm. Build these responses into your interactions, and anger will have fewer chances to leak out. Even if you are struggling with anger, being nice is not inauthentic—it is godly. Jesus asks us to love our enemies, do good to those who despitefully use us, and pray for those who persecute us.

> "But I say to you, love your enemies and pray for those who persecute you." **(Matthew 5:44)**

CALM-DOWN CARD—TAKING STEPS TO INCREASE THE GAP

When I first started to slow my anger down, it was all I could do to have a gap of a few seconds before I expressed my anger through my actions, face, or words. I created a card to read to keep the anger from taking over. I must have pulled out the card ten times the first few days to insert time and new thoughts into the process of resetting my anger. At times, it felt like I would never make progress in those early days, but using my calm-down card over and over again showed me that anger can be slowed down. Anger doesn't need to take over. Now, I have so many systems to refine my anger that it rarely reaches the surface of my face or into my words.

Let's create another calm-down card similar to the one from Day 2. We want to infuse more mental, emotional, and physical systems into your life so you can reduce the intensity of your anger and extract positive energy. You are creating a refinery, so you might think of these systems as pipes and processes to install in your mind that fit between your feelings and your mouth and/or body. Eventually, this series of systems will automatically re-route raw anger through these channels. But at the beginning, you will have to force yourself to work through these questions. Make a card or note on your phone to look at to slow down the rising anger. Carry it with you and work through it multiple times daily as needed. This refinery won't work unless you have it and use it.

1. **Examine your anger.**

    • Who or what are you angry about?

2. **Admit that you are angry for some reason.**

    • "I am feeling anger right now."

    • "I am being self-focused right now."

3. **Redirect your mind away from your feelings of anger.**

    • Think about your family, favorite sports team, or favorite activity.

4. **Relax your body.**

- Lower your shoulders, loosen your neck, and wiggle your legs.
- Relax your muscles.
- Take no action—say nothing, do nothing.

5. **Repeat a Scripture verse slowly and quietly. Pick one or two to memorize.**

- "Let everyone be quick to hear, slow to speak and slow to anger." (James 1:19)
- "Be angry but do not sin." (Ephesians 4:26)
- "One who is slow to anger has great understanding; But one who is quick-tempered exalts folly." (Proverbs 14:29)
- "Why are you angry and why has your countenance fallen? Sin is crouching right at the door and its desire is for you. But you must master it." (Genesis 4:6,7)

6. **Look for unrealistic expectations.**

- What were you expecting that is unrealistic?
- Smile or laugh or embrace its "unrealistic-ness."

7. **Pray for the time to evaluate your response.**

- "Lord Jesus, I need more time to respond wisely rather than emotionally."

8. **Listen rather than respond.**

- "That is interesting … tell me more."
- Ask questions instead of making statements.

9. **Ask God for positive, kind, controlled, and loving responses, such as:**

- "Thank you for that."
- "That is fascinating."
- "I am flooded right now; I will get back to you on that."

- "Help me understand what you are thinking."
- "That is a new perspective on this situation. I will need some time to properly evaluate those ideas."

10. **Act normal and serve others when some part of you is seething with anger.**

- Practice walking normally when a part of you is angry.
- Practice talking calmly when a part of you is full of rage.
- Practice helping others when some part of you wants to demand an apology.

REFINING YOUR ANGER

Dear Heavenly Father,

Right now, I am feeling angry. Help me to relax my body and keep my mouth shut. I am taking a deep, relaxing breath. I want your Spirit controlling me to be quick to hear, slow to speak, and slow to anger. Show me where I am being unrealistic in my expectations. Let me smile or laugh at my unreasonable expectations. Help me listen more intently to You and the person in front of me.

In Jesus's Name, Amen

"GOD CREATED US TO BE DIFFERENT FROM THE ANIMALS, SO HE GAVE US AN OVERRIDE SYSTEM TO ACT AND PLAN WISELY."

—Gil Stieglitz

DAY

DON'T LET THE LIZARD BRAIN TAKE OVER

Psalm 4:4-5

If you're going to reset your anger, knowing what you are dealing with is imperative. Understanding how anger works in the body and the solutions God provides to overcome it will help you do the refining work necessary to live calmly and peacefully.

Inside all of us is a super-rapid response system where preservation and protection are automatically programmed. There is no thinking, just reacting. This is called the "Lizard Brain," the most primitive, base part of our brain that warns us of danger and operates from basic animal instincts and emotions rather than well-thought-out actions and plans.[3] Fortunately for us, God created us to be different from the animals, and so He created an override system, but we have to develop it and use it wisely (Genesis 1:26-27).

To develop the override system, we need to slow down the automatic response of our reactive lizard mode and control it with our God-given higher functionality. If we cannot slow down the process of our feelings that activate our lizard brain, then we are at its mercy. One of the major ways to override our lizard-brain response system is to memorize, study, and meditate on Scriptures dealing with anger. There are powerful truths hidden in these anger-focused verses, and you can meditate on them (mull them over) to receive their insights and help.

One of the ways my youth pastor discipled me was to have me memorize and meditate on Scripture that dealt with the issues and problems I was facing. He would assign me verses and ask me to quote them back to him the following week. Then, he would ask me to meditate on these passages, and I'd show him my written pages of study and insights. His method changed me. He rewired my brain through Scripture. When he saw my repeated anger, he decided to have me start memorizing and meditating on Scriptures that dealt with anger and meekness. This book is the result of many hours of practicing biblical meditation on the verses he assigned. Now it's my turn to ask you to read these Scripture verses ten times out loud until you can say them without looking and meditating on what they tell you. They will work powerfully if they are a part of your subconscious mind.

"He who is slow to anger has great understanding, But he who is quick-tempered exalts folly."
(Proverbs 14:29)

"A hot-tempered man stirs up strife, But the slow to anger calms a dispute."
(Proverbs 15:18)

"Let no unwholesome word proceed from your mouth but only such a word as is good for edification."
(Ephesians 4:29)

THE PHYSICAL ASPECTS OF ANGER

Anger is a complex emotion that manifests in four different stages within our bodies and minds. Understanding these stages is essential for managing anger effectively.[4]

Stage 1: Triggering Event

Mirror neurons in the brain observe that things are not how we want them to be. This could be due to feeling disrespected, hurt, losing, or not getting our way. These observations trigger a cascade of emotional responses.

Stage 2: Limbic Response

The limbic brain, often called the "lizard brain," fires up to initiate change. It wants to get its own way. It prepares us to engage in attack mode to win at all costs. This primal response is designed to protect us but can lead to destructive behavior if not managed properly. It is natural to want to change everything to get our own way, but it cannot be let out in its primal form. It is like the unthinking lizard that will attack and bite.

Stage 3: Adrenal Response

Adrenal glands secrete hormones like adrenaline to provide the energy needed for this response. This surge of energy equips us for physical action but can also fuel our anger, making it harder to control. This is where the raw energy comes from, and refining it will help us make the changes needed to change ourselves, others, circumstances, and situations. We just have to refine this energy into a usable form for our situation.

Stage 4: Cognitive Control

God designed the prefrontal cortex to override the limbic system and the energy of the adrenal glands to keep us from doing anything rash or destructive. This section of the brain is in the front of the skull and surrounds the verbal processing center of the brain. Some people have an underdeveloped prefrontal cortex and cannot control their urges and impulses. This is typical of teenagers and young males before the age of twenty-five. Maturity means we should be able to keep our minds in charge even when we feel anger rising. This prefrontal cortex, when developed, helps us decide if it is the right time to act on our anger and what type of change is wise.

OVERRIDE THE LIZARD BRAIN WITH SCRIPTURE

In Psalm 4:4-5, King David, who was speaking under the inspiration of the Holy Spirit, describes how our body works with anger and how to keep wisdom in control. The apostle Paul memorized and meditated on this passage and wrote the Ephesians 4 passage on anger also under the inspiration of the Holy Spirit.

"Tremble, and do not sin; Meditate in your heart upon your bed, and be still. Selah. Offer the sacrifices of righteousness, And trust in the Lord."
(Psalm 4:4-5)

Using these verses from Psalm 4, let's apply each action to reset our anger.

1. Tremble, and do not sin
This means we can feel the anger but don't let it out. David uses a Hebrew word that means shake or tremble about the emotion inside of us. It can be anger. It could be grief. It could be fear or love. Strong emotions can make us tremble. Anger wants to get out and be in charge of what we say and do, but that would not be wise. King David and the apostle Paul say, "Feel the feeling, but don't let it out." They knew that if you do, it will be destructive or harmful in some way. This is what King David should have done with his feelings of sexual desire for Bathsheba, but he let it out, and it led to significant sin in his life and destruction in the country.

2. Meditate in your heart upon your bed
This phrase tells us we need to change the way we think about what upsets and irritates us. Anger has a perspective on what just happened, but there are other perspectives. King David wants us

to begin a mental and emotional process in which we evaluate our emotions before we let them out. Essentially, he suggests we set up a refinery and start using it. Not every strong emotion should be let out. Sometimes, when we are under the influence of strong emotions, we need to sit or lie down and feel the power of the emotion. We need to separate ourselves from this emotion flowing through our bodies. It is not us but the emotion; it wants to take over for us. As God says in Genesis 4:7 to Cain, sin is crouching at the door, and its desire is for us, but we must master it. We know that Cain did not master sin; he let his anger at God and his brother fully possess him. With anger in the driver's seat, Cain killed his brother, Abel, and forever changed the course of his life. He let anger take control, and it ruined him.

I am afraid for many people who have been told all their lives that they should let their hearts decide or allow their emotions to be in the driver's seat of their choices. It always leads to a diminished life in some dimension. God has given us emotions to add spice and energy to life but not to be the goal of life. All of us have all kinds of feelings and emotions flowing through our mind and soul on a daily basis. Be very careful about putting your feelings in charge of your words or actions.

3. And be still

This is saying that we may be aware of anger, but we don't have to let it out. God says to be still, or as the apostle Paul says in Romans 6, play dead. Our emotions have all kinds of instructions for us, but we don't need to obey what they say. We need to be still until we hear from God about what we should do, even repeating the words, "I am not angry." We are not ready to move until we know the wise course of action. In Romans 6, the apostle says that we should consider ourselves dead to our passions and desires but tell God we are ready to do what He tells us to do. We know that His will is better than the temporary pleasure our emotions can bring. "With God's help, I will not allow this feeling to possess my whole body." Be still long enough to play out the chess moves that anger and wisdom want to make.

4. Offer the sacrifices of righteousness

There will be sacrifices that the righteous will need to make to keep their emotions from taking over. Some activities might need to be sacrificed because they often fill us with rage. Some positive actions, activities, and words will need to be added to our lives because they encourage and energize us for a wise life. Some people might even need to be removed from our close friendship pool. Ask for God's help to stop doing some things and start doing new things. Create a delightful, peaceful, controlled life of positive impact, and eliminate the wild, destructive elements of your life that do not please God.

5. And trust in the LORD

There will be areas where the old success strategies we learned when we were ages nine to fourteen will have to be discarded. We get angry, but yelling at people will have to be replaced by us asking questions and dialoguing. We will have to trust God that letting other people express themselves will result in better relationships and more wisdom. Controlling people was our old way of ensuring we got our way. Now, we will have to trust God and know He has a greater plan for our lives.

When you begin to trust God with this anger-reset process, you will learn new ways of dealing with people and adjust to new ways of thinking, acting, and speaking. You'll be given the opportunity to ask questions and learn from others, and you will learn to trust that God will guide you when you don't know how things will turn out.

HOW TO COMMUNICATE WHEN YOU WANT TO BITE SOMEONE'S HEAD OFF

❑ Recognize your anger is trying to communicate in unhealthy ways, but you need to use words. (Proverbs 14:29)

❑ Realize that until you can calmly ask for positive change, the lizard brain is in charge.

❑ Let the emotion pass or be disconnected from your mind.

❑ Think about "Why am I upset?"

❑ Much anger is really about "I want my way." What is it you want to have happen?

❑ Think of three positive ways to ask for what you want.

❑ Practice communicating through positive words, questions, planning, discussions, and options. Slow down, take a breath, and ask:

> *Help me understand what you were thinking …*
>
> *Here is what I was thinking …*
>
> *Here is what I positively want …*

GETTING AWAY FROM AUTOMATIC ANGER

Dear Heavenly Father,

I admit I have a hard time not going into automatic anger when I don't get my way. That is not of You, Lord. You want me to renew my mind through Scripture and the Holy Spirit. Show me the positive ways I can calmly communicate what I want to have happen rather than fixating on what I don't want. Thank You for dying on the cross for my sins. I need You to help me be a redeemed, thinking human instead of a reactive lizard

In Jesus's Name, Amen

D A Y

CONFESS YOU HAVE A PROBLEM

1 John 1:9

When Bob (not his real name) admitted he could not control his anger on his own, it was a huge win. A weight dropped off his shoulders, and he was able to start learning how to be calm and peaceful. Whenever he was in charge of trying to handle his feelings of anger, he lost the battle most of the time. He needed a new strategy, which involved admitting that he needed help from God and others. If you are going to become calm, peaceful, and controlled, you will need to agree with God and others that you have been angry and it is wrong.

In this fifth anger-reset strategy, you will need to be honest about how you express anger in your life and the damage you have caused because of it. There is a cleansing that can happen here if you do this. God wants to forgive you for how you have damaged people, relationships, and your future because of your anger. But before you can sense the forgiveness of God, you will need to agree with Him that you have been angry and may have a habitual problem with anger. **Admitting you have a problem with anger means exploring all the ways it has leaked out in your life.** Maybe you can relate to some of these ways:

- Using anger to get your way

- Being bitter for years

- Being a volcanic rage machine when things upset you

- Being a screamer or yeller

- Being sarcastic and slanderous when you don't get what you want

- Enjoy planning how to get back at people who have hurt you

During parts of my journey to manage anger, I found I had to apologize to my family at least every other week, admitting I was wrong. I admitted that my anger was wrong, and I asked them to forgive me. It cleared the air and kept our relationship strong and growing. If I had tried to cover it up and pretend I was not angry or expressed it was all their fault, then our relationship would have been fractured. Yes, they needed to do some things differently, but I needed to express my reaction, training, and correction in calm and controlled ways. If you are willing to be humble enough to admit you are wrong, it opens new ways to control your anger.

Confession is agreeing with God about reality. Denial is pretending we are not angry … that we are not bitter … that we don't feel like screaming when we do. We can't fully reset our anger until we admit we are angry in some form. You don't have to let it out, but you do have to acknowledge it is there prompting you. It can be so freeing to admit that you are angry. Today, you can stop living in denial and confess, "I am angry."

Yes, I am angry at this person for doing that to me.

Yes, I am bitter about what happened to me fifteen years ago, and I want them to pay.

Yes, I don't like what they are pressuring me to do, so I am constantly sarcastic and slanderous toward them.

Yes, I am seething inside about what someone did to me, and I have plans to block them or do harm to them.

Realize that anger in and of itself is not the problem; it's letting it out in damaging ways. A number of years ago, I was dealing with a leader about to get fired over his anger issues. He would throw staplers when things didn't go his way. He would spin donuts in the parking lot to let off steam. He thought that because he was such a good leader in other areas of the business and the business was growing, everyone was overlooking this problem. They weren't, and it was affecting the whole organization. He kept trying to deny he had a problem with anger, and nothing changed for him until he confessed he had one.

I remember a young mother who developed a hoarse and raspy voice because she was trying to control her children through yelling and screaming. She would tell you that she was not an angry person, but she was constantly angry at her boys. She adamantly refused to learn any new parenting strategies beyond yelling and screaming what she wanted. It didn't work, and it destroyed her voice and her marriage in the process. I don't want that for you; I want you to learn to confess your anger so change can occur.

THERE ARE SIX TYPES OF ANGER THE BIBLE ADDRESSES

The Bible tells us anger can take at least six different forms. Look at each type and see if you are guilty of trying to get your way through that form of anger. Then, go through each type of anger, read the explanation, and look up what the Bible says about it. Make notes in the margin or a journal.

TYPE OF ANGER	EXPLANATION	SCRIPTURE
Anger	This is rage rising within you that wants something to change.	James 1:20; 4:1-3
Bitterness	This is lack of forgiveness. This is wanting vengeance. This is festering hurt.	Matthew 6:12; Romans 12:19

TYPE OF ANGER	EXPLANATION	SCRIPTURE
Wrath	This is full external rage, the volcano that is spewing until it is all out.	Colossians 3:8; 1 Timothy 2:8
Clamor	This is yelling, screaming, and making noise, a loud harsh sound.	Ephesians 4:31–32 (KJV); Titus 2:2, 11–12
Slander	This is sarcasm. This is quiet anger that tries to get back by making comments, put downs, and even contempt.	Leviticus 19:16; Psalm 15:3; Proverbs 10:18; Proverbs 29:8; Matthew 15:19; 2 Corinthians 12:20
Malice	This is the plan to get even, to pay back. This is hidden harm aimed at your enemy.	1 Corinthians 5:8; 1 Peter 2:1; Titus 3:3

Looking at these descriptions, what type of anger is your go-to response? What stood out to you in the Scriptures? Are you ready to confess?

CONFESS YOUR ANGER TO GOD

Beware! Anger wants to trap you in the past. The truth of the matter is that you cannot be transformed into your full God-given potential by dragging the hatred and pain of the past with you. But anger does everything possible to keep you stuck in the past—past hurts, disappointments, guilt, shame, the works. Anger wants to plot revenge. It doesn't want to forget and move on; it wants to dredge up the hurts of the past. Anger creates a plan to wound and destroy. This is why it is so important to overcome your anger.

God wants a good and abundant life for you, so you cannot let the past define your future. You cannot have all the good things of the future built on top of a toxic waste dump of bitterness, anger, hatred, and pain. You must learn to release this, or it will destroy your potential.

The way you release anger is through confession. Many people find that admitting to the Lord that they are feeling angry or bitter or wanting to scream is very helpful in controlling their anger. It is important to realize that just because we feel anger, it is not the whole of us. We can choose to act on different impulses. If you think of anger as a temptation, just like lust or greed, it may take control of your whole person sometimes, but it is not the whole of you. When we admit what is happening in us, we can use the systems we have collected to diffuse our emotions. You may have to agree with God that you are angry five times in one day (or, like me, ten times a day); you can ask for His help in not making that kind of angry choice in the future. It's okay; He's listening and gladly accepting your confession. He knows your confession is a critical part of the path.

A thorough confession looks like this:

❑ Admit to the Lord directly that you are _____(angry, wrathful, bitter, screaming, slanderous, sarcastic, or malicious). Tell Him what you have been or are angry about right now.

❏ Admit to God what you are angry about. Tell Him what you wanted and didn't get. If you don't know, ask Him to reveal it to you.

❏ Ask for His forgiveness, which is in Christ Jesus. You need His power, grace, and mercy so the damage of your anger won't destroy relationships or your potential.

❏ Thank Him for the death of Christ in your place to forgive your selfish focus. Appreciate what God has done for you. He empowered you after you messed up and absorbed your punishment for you.

❏ Ask Him to make you a calm and controlled person who does not let your anger, frustration, or rage destroy people, relationships, and future potential. You must want His goal of being a calm, controlled, and peaceful person rather than using your anger to get your way. Life is better His way! Use all the energy He gives you to accomplish His purposes for His glory.

CONFESSING ANGER

Dear Heavenly Father,

I admit that I am angry right now. I often cannot control my anger and say and do things I shouldn't. I act before I think, and I want that to change. I need you to be in me, with me, over me, and through me. Please, Lord Jesus, come into my life at a new level and save me from my own destructive reactions. Show me how to walk a controlled, calm, and impactful life.

In Jesus's Name, Amen

"MY ANGER IS ALMOST ALWAYS CONNECTED TO MY EXPECTATIONS."

—Gil Stieglitz

D A Y

UNDERSTAND YOUR
UNREALISTIC EXPECTATIONS

James 4:1

Did you know that almost all anger comes from unrealistic expectations? I was driving to the airport several years ago, and I was running a little late. As I was pulling into the parking lot, I saw a shuttle bus coming around, and the timing would be perfect. I imagined that I would jump out of the car, grab my stuff from the back seat, and the bus would be right there waiting for me. I would jump on board and get whisked to the terminal, making up time and getting on the flight with no problem. But ... when I grabbed my stuff from the car's back seat, one of the straps on my bag got caught on the headrest, and I couldn't get the bag out of the car. I pulled harder and harder as I saw the bus getting ready to leave because I was not walking toward it. I got madder and madder with this stupid bag holding up my perfect plan. The bus took off, and now I was going to be late. Why couldn't the driver have waited for me? Didn't he see I was coming? I was so mad.

It didn't take long before I started laughing. I realized it was completely unrealistic for the whole airport to adjust to help me make my flight. My ridiculous expectation was that the air traffic controller would somehow see me pulling into the parking lot, struggling with my bag. He would call the shuttle bus driver and the pilot, telling them, "Gil is struggling with his bag; just wait for him. He is too important to miss the bus or flight." I laughed all the way to the terminal, and guess what? The plane had not taken off yet, and I was in a good mood.

I was talking with a young woman the other day, and she was complaining about her workplace. It was horribly disorganized, and the people in charge did not communicate well with the employees. Even when they said they would do something, they didn't. Even when they said they would organize something, they didn't. She was getting increasingly upset because they did not do what they said they would do and what everyone knew was the right thing.

"What should I do?" she asked.

"Would you mind if I gave you a different perspective?" I knew what I would tell her wouldn't necessarily be what she wanted to hear, but the answer was clear to me.

"Yes," she said eagerly.

"You have been telling me that this company, the boss, and your co-workers do not communicate as they should for the whole time you have been at this company," I said. "You also told me they have even agreed with you on many occasions that they are not as organized as they need to be. Therefore, your expectation that they would communicate and be organized is unrealistic. They have never shown you before they can be organized how you want them to be. So why would it be realistic to expect them to start doing these things right now? What you expect may be the right way to run a company, but this company will never do that. You need to stop expecting what they have clearly demonstrated is beyond them. Your choices are to either live with their lack of communication and organization or find a new job. Don't get mad because they can't meet your expectations. They have shown you that they never will."

This changed her perspective completely. She went on about her life and decided to put aside her unrealistic expectations. No longer did she expect them to do things they were incapable of doing. She did look at other places to work but chose to stay because of the good people she knew. She did have to be reminded on occasion that it was unrealistic to expect them to communicate effectively or organize themselves fully. Still, she no longer let it get her to the point of anger. She continued working there and had a great time.

Think about what makes you angry—does this describe your thinking?

"I don't get angry when I hope something will happen."

"I don't get angry if I wish things would happen a certain way."

"I don't get angry if I have a dream of how things could be."

"But I do get angry if I expect something to go a certain way, and it doesn't happen."

My anger is almost always connected to my expectations. Although the expectations may be right or even good, are they unrealistic considering my preparation, planning, communication, circumstances, and the people involved? Now, because of my anger-control training, I have learned to laugh when I feel anger rising in me. My impossible wants have turned into expectations really fast.

I was talking with a young couple the other day who are raising very young children. They are doing a marvelous job, but it is frustrating at times. The husband said, "Why won't they just listen?" I laughed, then said, "It is unrealistic to expect that telling your kids once or even a dozen times will result in them doing what you asked." He expected the kids to hear what he said and do a great job of obeying the first time. He needed to find other ways of teaching than just talking, maybe more training, more demonstrating, making them try, and asking them what they should do before the event. The key idea here is that his anger meant that he had an unrealistic expectation of what would happen with raising his young kids. He knew them, but he still had an unrealistic expectation of how they would react to his telling them what to do. (For more parenting techniques, I invite you to read *Wise Parenting: Creating the Joy of Family* to help your family become the best it can be.)

I would get mad when I played golf because my ball kept slicing to the right. But since that is what my golf ball did 90 percent of the time, I had an unrealistic expectation that the ball would fly straight. It rarely went straight, but because it did a few times, I began to expect that it should. How stupid! My anger was born out of my bad expectations. Much of your anger is also born from your enormous, unrealistic expectations.

I watch many wives and husbands get angry because they expect their marriage partner to do things they clearly can't or won't do. Everyone has strengths and weaknesses. If your partner has a weakness in an area, then it is unrealistic to expect them to operate well in that area. Couples come up to me and ask, "Don't you think that my husband or wife should do a particular thing?" In many cases, I told them it may be the right thing to expect, but it may be beyond their spouse's current abilities. They need to work with their spouse instead of demanding they be perfect. (I am not talking about immorality or violence.) Many couples also expect their spouse to read their mind. That is an unrealistic expectation as well. We must communicate clearly and calmly if we want them to know what we are thinking.

Below is a list of things that have made me angry over the years. Do you relate to any of these unrealistic expectations?

- ❑ I get mad when people get in my way on the freeway.
- ❑ I get mad when my sports team doesn't win.
- ❑ I get mad when I carry too much, and one thing drops and breaks.
- ❑ I get mad when someone interrupts me to correct something I say.
- ❑ I get mad when I do not win a game.

- ❑ I get mad when I am in a hurry and bump into a wall or injure myself somehow.
- ❑ I get mad when I don't get an A on a test.
- ❑ I get mad when the kids do not do what I tell them to do.
- ❑ I get mad when my spouse doesn't read my mind.
- ❑ I get mad when people at work don't do what I suggest.
- ❑ I get mad when people don't act like I think they should.
- ❑ I get mad when people don't listen to me.
- ❑ I get mad when I trip over something I didn't see.
- ❑ I get mad when there isn't an open parking spot for me.

I experienced all of these anger episodes, which were born out of unrealistic expectations and triggered anger inside of me. I've grown to realize that anger signals an unrealistic expectation in my life. I need to not give in to expressing my anger externally but look at my expectations. I need to change the expectations to a wish, a dream, a desire, or something much more realistic.

ARE YOUR EXPECTATIONS UNREALISTIC?

Each unrealistic expectation is usually about someone else, a situation, life in general, or something else. If you are mad, there is an unrealistic expectation somewhere. First, you need to find what you have allowed to harden into an expectation. Then, you need to come to grips with why it is unrealistic.

Think through the last three times you were angry. What was the expectation? Was it unrealistic?

1.

2.

3.

Ask yourself these types of questions:

Why is this expectation unrealistic?

Is it because I didn't communicate?

Is it because I didn't plan?

Is it unrealistic because I am not God?

Is it unrealistic because life doesn't always work like I want?

Is it unrealistic because I don't have the skills to pull off my expectations?

Is it unrealistic because I didn't allow enough time?

Is it unrealistic because I didn't study hard enough?

Is it unrealistic because I am not in charge?

When I read these questions, I can see what I expected to happen. Now, I often laugh because I can see that what I expected is impossible, and I know I was stupid for thinking it could happen.

Scripture says that we fight, quarrel, and have conflicts because we want something that will not happen. Our pleasures have begun to expect certain things. They get angry and lash out when they don't get what they want.

"What is the source of quarrels and conflicts among you? Is not the source your pleasures that wage war in your members?"
(James 4:1)

Your anger reveals there are unrealistic expectations, so you can start the process of examining, adjusting, and redirecting them. Look at these areas where you tend to get angry and see what unrealistic expectations begin to surface:

- Freeway
- Kids
- Spouse
- Work
- Government
- Bosses (people in authority over you)
- Friends

- Neighbors
- Need to win

ANGER MANAGEMENT TRUTHS

My friend Kevin A. Thompson has a great book called *Stay in Your Lane*. I highly recommend the book. It tells us the truth that there are only three columns everything in life falls into:

1. Stuff you control and can change.

2. Stuff someone else controls and can change.

3. Stuff only God controls and can change.[5]

Pastor Thompson finds that many people come to him and want him to tell them the secret of changing another person or changing God. He always graciously lets them know we don't have control over those things. You can only change what you can change. Throughout this process of overcoming anger, repeat these truths about your role in controlling your anger:

I must stop expecting others to behave as I would in the same situation.

I must stop assuming that if something is easy for me, then it should be easy for them.

I must realize I see the world through my perspectives, assumptions, background, victories, and defeats. These are grossly unrealistic expectations for everyone else.

I can only change what I can change.

Begin the process of making your expectations more realistic and do what you can do. I guarantee the world will become a much less frustrating place.

CALM-DOWN CARD: RESETTING EXPECTATIONS

If you struggle with unrealistic expectations, like I did and still sometimes do, create a calm-down card with these five truths and use it whenever you get angry. Once you realize that your expectations for this person in this situation are unrealistic, you can begin to laugh at your stupid expectations and let go of your anger. You can embrace and reset to a more realistic expectation for this situation or this person.

If you are angry, then ...

1. Realize you may be expecting something unrealistic. Ask:

   ❑ What is the expectation?

   ❑ Is it right?

   ❑ Is it needed?

   ❑ Is it unrealistic with this person or in this situation?

2. How is that expectation unrealistic with this person or in this situation?

3. What is a realistic expectation with this person or in this situation?

4. How could your expectations become realistic in the future?

5. Should you abandon this expectation and adjust to reality?

HELP WITH UNREALISTIC EXPECTATIONS

Dear Heavenly Father,

I have all kinds of unrealistic expectations that trigger anger in me. I cannot expect others to read my mind or the world to revolve around me. Please help me realize when my expectations are unrealistic. Show me how to manage or change my expectations. Show me how to bring about righteous change. Show me how to accept and adapt to other people's expectations and behaviors.

In Jesus's Name, Amen

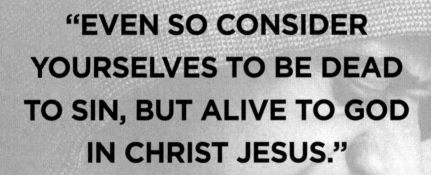

"EVEN SO CONSIDER YOURSELVES TO BE DEAD TO SIN, BUT ALIVE TO GOD IN CHRIST JESUS."

—Romans 6:11

D A Y

LEARN TO PLAY DEAD

Romans 6:1–4, 11–14

Learning to play dead to anger is one of the key strategies for defeating temptations of all kinds. The New Testament describes this process, which we must master if we truly want to control our anger.

When I was in high school, my battle with anger issues was at its peak. To help me, my youth pastor would make me lie down on the floor and play dead while quoting Romans 6:1–4, 11–14. After that, he would have me turn in ten pages of biblical meditation on these crucial verses about defeating temptation. It was a rigorous exercise, but I knew my life would not get better if I didn't take what he was suggesting seriously. So I did, and I hope you will as well.

> What shall we say then? Are we to continue in sin so that grace may increase? May it never be! How shall we who died to sin still live in it? Or do you not know that all of us who have been baptized into Christ Jesus have been baptized into His death? Therefore we have been buried with Him through baptism into death, so that as Christ was raised from the dead through the glory of the Father, so we too might walk in newness of life. …

Even so consider yourselves to be dead to sin, but alive to God in Christ Jesus. Therefore do not let sin reign in your mortal body so that you obey its lusts, and do not go on presenting the members of your body to sin as instruments of unrighteousness; but present yourselves to God as those alive from the dead, and your members as instruments of righteousness to God. For sin shall not be master over you, for you are not under law but under grace. (Romans 6:1-4, 11-14 NASB)

When I had finished quoting the Scriptures, lying down with my eyes closed, my pastor would then say, "Now I want you to keep your eyes closed and play dead. You can't move because you are dead. You can't open your eyes; you are dead. You can't reach up and grasp anything; you are dead. Now imagine in this dead state that ten beautiful naked women are marching over you. What happens? 'Nothing because I am dead' is the answer I am looking for. You can't open one eye and look. You can't reach up and touch. You are completely nonresponsive."

Then he would say, "Now imagine that one hundred dollar bills are marching over you. What happens? 'Nothing because I am dead' is the answer I am looking for." Then he would say, "Now imagine that someone who really makes you angry is marching over to you. What do you do? 'Nothing because I am dead' is the answer I am looking for." Trust me, it took me a while before I no longer said, "I would jump up and punch the guy," but I eventually got there.

My pastor knew that I needed to grasp this playing-dead concept if the gap between stimulus and response was to grow. I needed to create time to hear from God about other responses than what I would naturally do. I needed time to look at various options for what to do when I was being prompted to anger, lust, pride, greed, or whatever. I learned quickly that I had about 120 seconds to play dead to the anger before I would pop the clutch, and my mouth and body would start moving. I have found that God speaks in that gap.

When I ask God, "What do you want me to do instead of how I want to respond?" He usually puts a picture in my mind of something He wants me to do instead of what I want to do. It could be a vacuum cleaner, a pile of dirty dishes, a phone call to someone, going on a run, or a change in activity. If I act on what the Holy Spirit is prompting, I beat the temptation. If I pause too long and think about the anger, lust, greed, sloth, or whatever, then I give into the sin.

In modern psychology, this is the gap between stimulus and response. Creating a gap between when we are stimulated and before we actually do something is essential. The bigger we can make this gap, the more freedom we will have, and the more transformation will take place in us. Stephen Covey explains, "Between stimulus and response, there is space. In that space lies our freedom and power to choose our response. In our response lies our growth and our happiness."[6]

When we learn to make the gap bigger and bigger, this is how you slow down your anger. This is how you have the time to be wise. Playing dead or being nonresponsive is one of the clear signs of maturity. Can you hold feelings of fear in your life without letting them dominate your life? Can you hold feelings of anger without letting them dominate your life? Are you able to have selfish feelings but not let them dictate what you do and say? You must find ways of acting and speaking that are loving, peaceful, patient, and kind that do not tap into or show the frustration, bitterness, or anger inside of you. (See Galatians 5:13-26.)

When I first started trying to play dead, I could hold off action for about two minutes, meaning I needed to redirect my actions within that time. Now, I can put aside the stimulus for days and return to it when I have more wisdom and clarity over the situation. Please understand:

It is in this gap that you have free choice.

It is in this gap that you can insert wisdom.

It is in this gap that you can hear the Holy Spirit.

Some have described this process as pushing in the clutch so that the engine runs at a high rate, but the car does not move. Your internal life may be spinning at a high rate, but you are not saying anything or doing anything that engages that anger. You become nonresponsive to the other person and your own feelings.

The goal is to become the kind of person who may be stimulated to anger but who does not allow anger to dominate or show in their body. Anyone who masters this process may have something that is really bugging them, but they can carry on normal conversations and be nice to people. They know that they will deal with the situation or person later. They will not let their response be immediate or uncontemplated.

PLAYING DEAD EXERCISE

Take the time to physically act out dying to the temptation and sin that is in your world. Die with Christ in His tomb. All your old stimuli and response arrangements are now ended because you are dead. Listen to the voice of the Holy Spirit.

- ❑ Lay down on the floor on your back like you are dead.
- ❑ Quote Romans 6:1-4, 11-14 out loud.
- ❑ Think of a situation or a person who makes you angry. Imagine taking no action because you are dead.
- ❑ Say nothing. You are dead. You cannot speak. You can't say or think of snide comments.
- ❑ Relax your body. You are dead. You cannot respond to this person or situation.
- ❑ Await further instruction. Know that God wants to direct you so you don't sin by expressing your anger, frustration, bitterness, or malice.
- ❑ Ask God for His instruction. What does He want you to do? Listen for a new thought, idea, a picture of what to do, or a Scripture verse that comes to mind.

LENGTHEN YOUR PLAYING DEAD TIME

Continue working to create a bigger gap between stimulus and response. Sometimes, I will create a gap of days after I get upset at something my wife or one of my kids does, and then after days, God whispers, "Let this go. It is not worth bringing it up." Sometimes, I will wait days, and then the Lord will whisper, "Bring it up now from a positive point of view. This is important for strengthening this relationship." Eventually, you will realize that you can create, with God's help, a big enough gap between stimulus and response as you want or need.

Next time you get angry, try one or more of these ideas to create a gap big enough to allow you to respond in God's way.

- ❏ Do the righteous ideas that flow into your mind during the gap
- ❏ Walk away
- ❏ Say, "I am flooded right now; I need a minute."
- ❏ Smile because of the unrealistic expectations you have
- ❏ Do what God suggests
- ❏ Do a workout—go for a walk, run, push-ups, or whatever you can do
- ❏ Lie down
- ❏ Pray
- ❏ Call a friend

PLAYING DEAD TO ANGER

Dear Heavenly Father,

I am feeling angry right now and need to disconnect from those feelings. I am relaxing my body to give me time to hear from You. Lord Jesus, I need to know what You want me to say or do instead of letting this feeling tell me what to do. I will listen to Your voice. I will do what You suggest. I am listening.

In Jesus's Name, Amen

"TO WIN AGAINST ANGER, WE NEED LOTS OF VITAMIN S AND THE HELP OF THE HOLY SPIRIT."

—Gil Stieglitz

D A Y

8

ADD MORE VITAMIN S

Psalm 1:1–3

Several years ago, scientists discovered certain vitamins are keys to our physical bodies' flourishing. They found that without these little compounds, we would wither and become disease-prone even if we ate well. We need vitamins to be healthy, and fortunately, we have discovered all kinds of vitamins that do all kinds of things to allow the body to thrive.

One thing our spiritual lives need is Vitamin S or Scripture. Without a sufficient amount of God's Word, we will not be able to resist temptation and become our whole, abundant Christian selves. I watch people regularly attend church, listen to sermons, watch Christian television shows and movies, and pray, but they do not grow stronger each year. Instead, they are weak and discouraged, wondering why their lives aren't going how they want.

I believe they struggle because they do not have enough Vitamin S in them. Yes, they believe in Jesus for the forgiveness of their sins, but they don't get nourishment from the word of God. They are not strong enough to live vibrant Christian lives and follow the guidance of the Holy Spirit. It's not enough to have Scripture topically applied to us for us; we must take it in and digest it into our innermost being.

Psalm 1:1-3 describes the relationship between this blessed person and God's Word:

Blessed is the one who does not walk in step with the wicked or stand in the way that sinners take or sit in the company of mockers, but whose delight is in the law of the LORD, and who meditates on his law day and night. That person is like a tree planted by streams of water, which yields its fruit in season and whose leaf does not wither—whatever they do prospers.

(Psalm 1:1-3 NIV)

You can see from this passage that the blessed person meditates on God's Word day and night—they delight in it and prosper as a result. If you and I are going to win against anger, then we will need lots of Vitamin S working inside of us with the help of the Holy Spirit. We need to be strengthened in our inner man to glorify Christ.

My youth pastor was relentless in getting me to read Scripture. He changed my life. If he saw a problem in my life, he would assign me several passages to memorize, study, and meditate upon. He would make me quote the verses back to him. He would make me show him my meditations and study notes on the passages. The word of God got into my life and changed how I thought about everything. I would highly recommend taking in much more Vitamin S. Here is the kind of list my youth pastor would give me on issues regarding anger (NASB):

"But everyone must be quick to hear, slow to speak and slow to anger."

(James 1:19)

"The anger of man does not achieve the righteousness of God."
(James 1:20)

"Cease from anger and forsake wrath; Do not fret; it leads only to evildoing."
(Psalm 37:8)

"Be still, and know that I am God."
(Psalm 46:10 NIV)

"Set a guard, O LORD, over my mouth; Keep watch over the door of my lips."
(Psalm 141:3)

"Be angry, and yet do not sin; do not let the sun go down on your anger."
(Ephesians 4:26)
bitterness and wrath and anger and clamor and slander be put away from you, along with all malice."
(Ephesians 4:31)

"But now you also, put them all aside: anger, wrath, malice, slander, and abusive speech from your mouth."
(Colossians 3:8)

Don't just read these verses. Memorize them, study them, and meditate on them. They will change you. If you want to understand the spiritual discipline of biblical meditation more, I encourage you to read my books *Spiritual Disciplines of a C.H.R.I.S.T.I.A.N.* and They Laughed When I Wrote Another Book about Prayer. Many people have been helped by the instruction they provide.

One of the interesting things about the temptations of anger, ego, lust, greed, envy, or sloth is that they come from "noise" in our heads. We often do not realize these "noises" are lying to us. They are not whispering success strategies but addiction pathways that will trap us in destructive cycles. We must resist the noise and listen for the voice of the Holy Spirit, who will guide us to be successful and relaxed.

Actually, I do want you to add more noise inside your head, but I want it to be Scripture because it is God's words—the "noise" the Holy Spirit uses to talk to you. The more you slowly repeat Scripture, confess Scripture, personalize Scripture, mentally rehearse Scripture, draw Scripture, sing Scripture, and journal Scripture, the more the Holy Spirit can speak clearly to you. This is especially true in the moments of temptation when it is hard to hear Him. Scripture pumps up the volume, and you'll know without a doubt whose voice is speaking to you.

PERSONALIZE SCRIPTURE BY READING OR WRITING IT OUT

Personalizing Scripture is very effective in engendering God's Word in your heart. To practice this discipline, insert your name and the sin you are being tempted to commit into Romans 6. Read these out loud, then write them in your journal or the blanks provided.

What shall you say then _____? Are you to continue being angry that grace may increase to you? May it never be. How can you who died to anger still live in it? Don't you know _____ that everyone who has been baptized into Christ has been baptized into His death?

Know this, _____, that your old self full of anger, pride, and lust was crucified with Him, in order that your anger might be done away with, so that you would no longer be a slave of anger; for he who has died is freed from anger.

Even so_____consider yourself dead to anger but alive to God in Christ Jesus. Therefore _____, do not let anger reign in your mortal body so that you obey its lusts. And _____, do not go on presenting the members of your body to anger as tools of destruction; but present yourself to God as those alive from the dead. For anger _____ shall not be master over you, for you are not under law but under grace.

CALM-DOWN CARD—THINK ... BREATHE ... RECITE SCRIPTURE IN YOUR MIND AND OUT LOUD

- Pick a Scripture verse from the list above and write it on a 3" x 5" card.

- Slowly recite it quietly or even under your breath as you try to slow down your anger.

- Breathe in ...

- Breathe out, quoting the Scripture ...

- Do this five more times.

- Practice doing this whenever you feel anger rising inside you.

ALLOW SCRIPTURE TO REWIRE YOUR MIND

Dear Heavenly Father,

I admit I cannot control my anger on my own. I need more Vitamin S to rewire how I respond to anger. Please, Lord Jesus, remind me of the Scripture verses I need now and redirect my anger's energy. Thank You for dying on the cross for my sins. Bring Scripture to my mind when I need it. I will listen. Let me speak out Scripture rather than my rantings of anger.

In Jesus's Name, Amen

"WE MUST REMOVE SITUATIONS, PEOPLE, AND ACTIVITIES THAT CONSISTENTLY MAKE US STUMBLE IN OUR ANGER."

—Gil Stieglitz

DAY

CUT OFF YOUR RIGHT HAND

Matthew 5:29-30

The other day, I talked with a young businessman who is trying hard to work on his anger. He is making tremendous strides, saying he has reduced his anger by 40 percent. He asked me if he just needed to make the confession and use the calm-down cards until he no longer got angry. "No!" I told him. "You may be doing a good job of reducing your excessive anger, but now you need to go to the other side of your anger … stopping it before it shows up or begins welling up inside you." He now needed to begin the hard work of eliminating his anger before it began.

To get to this other side of anger, I explained how he would have to get rid of some of the things that consistently led him to anger, like watching sports, drinking alcohol, playing sports, and waiting until the last minute to do certain things. He would likely have to cut off ties with certain people and avoid certain triggering situations. Permanent sacrifices would have to be made if he were to eliminate certain parts of his anger. Look at the powerful way Jesus states this principle in Matthew 5:

If your right eye makes you stumble, tear it out and throw it from you; for it is better for you to lose one of the parts of your body, than for your whole body to be thrown into hell. If your right hand makes you stumble, cut it off and throw it from you; for it is better for you to lose one of the parts of your body, than for your whole body to go into hell. (Matthew 5:29-30 NASB)

Jesus is not literally telling us to cut off our hands or pluck out our eyes. He means we are to remove situations, people, and activities that consistently make us stumble. If something or someone constantly makes you angry, depressed, lustful, drunk, or some other negative action, then they or it may need to be cut out of your life. You say, "But I like doing that!" It doesn't matter. If it is destroying your God-given potential or your current life, get rid of it. You and I will have to be ruthless with some things we like doing but are putting us in a bad place. To win in life, we all have to make sacrifices. We sometimes have to stop doing some of the things we love that are derailing us from the goals we want to reach.

I know many people who have had to give up all alcohol because it surfaces issues and addictions that take them from their goals.

I know people who have had to stop going to certain types of shows because desires and habit patterns surface that destroy the progress they are making.

I know people who cannot be around certain kinds of music because it brings up situations and actions from their past that they never want to revisit.

Grow in every area you can. Process your anger and why it is there, realizing that you may have to eliminate some activities and situations that consistently surface anger in you. Everyone understands the concept of sacrifice in sports, business, family, and finances, but we tend to forget that this principle is also true in personal development. Decide what things you will give up to get where you want to go, and you will end up glorifying God in the process.

A number of years ago, I found myself regularly getting upset whenever I played basketball with my friends. I tried all of the other techniques talked about in this book. I just couldn't keep my frustration with certain basketball moves by other players from boiling over. I was talking with the Lord about the issue, and He immediately took me to Jesus's radical discussion about plucking out your eye and cutting off your right hand. After some discussion with God, I thought about what He was saying. I realized that playing basketball was one of those areas I needed to stop doing. I needed to cut off this unneeded source of frustration and anger if I wanted to move forward in my life. Basketball was a problem for me, and that whole area of anger and frustration is now gone because I no longer play. Sure, I am still active in other sports and exercise a lot, but I don't do the primary activity that seems to surface anger I cannot contain. Cutting something out of your life may not solve every area of anger, but it may be a solution that God directs you to implement.

I have watched the Tour de France bicycle race on television for years. I love riding my bike for long distances, but what these professionals do is extraordinary. They ride over three thousand miles in three weeks. That's a grueling one hundred miles almost every day. What we don't often see are the sacrifices these young men make to be really good at their sport. They give up time with family. They give up pizza and dessert. They give up a comfortable life with TV and outings. They give up a normal life to excel at this sport. To be the best in the world, they must give up some things. The same is true for Olympic athletes in any sport. They sacrifice all kinds of things for years to be the best and win the prize.

I remember one friend of mine who was trying to be a hammer thrower. He was really good, but he wasn't big enough. He had to eat ten times what he normally would to get big enough to compete with the elite hammer throwers. He used to tell me how sick he was of having to eat so much. He won some smaller competitions and had a shot at the Olympics, but in the end, he did not make it. He just couldn't get big enough. As soon as the goal was gone, he stopped eating vast quantities of food, and he shrunk and became a third of himself. I hardly recognized him the first time I saw him after his competing days were over.

The point is that if we are going to win against anger, we will have to make many sacrifices. We will need to remove some things and add some new things. However, the goal of pleasing the Lord Jesus and becoming all we can be is worth these sacrifices. If you and I are going to fulfill the dreams, goals, and ideas that God and we have about our lives, then we will need to say NO to some things and some people. We will also need to say YES to some people and some things. What is God calling you to cut off so you can be free from anger, frustration, bitterness, malice, and rage? I have found that certain people consistently trigger anger in me, so I limit or eliminate time with them. I may be able to handle them later when I am more mature or in a different place in my life, but right now, I cannot handle what they bring to me.

MAKING SACRIFICES TO RESET YOUR ANGER

1. What must you remove from your life to control your anger? Is God calling you to cut out some aspect of an area so you are no longer tempted to get angry? Looking at this list, think if any of these or aspects of them regularly make you angry:

   • sports
   • alcohol
   • driving
   • music
   • certain people
   • certain topics
   • certain activities
   • politics
   • time pressures
   • other

2. What will you sacrifice to get the life you've always wanted? Write your list of Who, What, and When.

   • Who makes you angry regularly? How can you avoid them or cut them out of your life?
   • What are the circumstances or situations that regularly make you angry? How can you avoid or cut out those circumstances or situations?
   • When do you find yourself getting the most angry? How can you avoid or stop doing certain things during that "angry" time?

ELIMINATE ANGER TRIGGERS

Dear Heavenly Father,

Please show me what or who triggers my anger. Who or what should I cut out of my life? What circumstances, situations, and people regularly trigger anger in me? Please come into my life at a new level and save me from my own destructive reactions. Show me how to cut these angry things out of my life. Thank You for dying on the cross for my sins. Enter into me and allow me to be calm.

In Jesus's Name, Amen

D A Y

ACQUIRE WISDOM, ACQUIRE UNDERSTANDING

Proverbs 4:5; Proverbs 17:27

Solomon tells us that his father, King David, repeatedly emphasized that he needed to find wisdom and understanding (Proverbs 4:3–6).[7] Of all the things he heard growing up, this idea stuck with him. David's message to his beloved son was, "You have to get beyond just thinking about what you want; you need to know how things are connected."

If you are angry, it indicates that you are not being wise or understanding. Anger requires a self-focused perspective; we can't see clearly when we're in the middle of it. Most of the time, our anger rises because of ignorance, a lack of planning, or not realizing how certain things are connected. So, what other perspectives and information would quiet this anger and frustration? Realize **there are solutions that your anger does not know about, so it's up to you to find them.** Things are much more connected than you know, so figure out how to connect them.

One of the consistent things I hear about that makes people really angry is when employers look at their potential new employees' social media pages. If the employer sees a person partying and doing wild and inappropriate things, they do not hire that person. Things are connected. If you are angry, it's likely you don't realize that some things are connected that you think are disconnected.

Every parent has regrets when raising their children, one of which is being angry at their children for something minor or stupid. Our kids don't need our anger directed at them for every little thing; they need to see us growing in wisdom and understanding. We can work to lessen our anger and instead grow wiser. Limit your regrets by asking more questions, listening to other perspectives, including your child's, and taking the time to think before acting or yelling.

What are other ways to see this situation so that everyone can win?

What can I do to allow everyone to win?

Who can give me a different perspective on this?

Where can I get new information about this situation?

What will happen after I make this decision?

One of the most important anger-reset techniques is to become wiser and acquire understanding. How often have you said, "If I had only known then what I know now, I would have acted differently"? When we say this, we are saying we lack knowledge, understanding, and wisdom. Our anger dissipates with new information, connections, and a broader perspective. Slow the process of anger by looking for these things. Seek wisdom from God and understanding from others before you act or speak.

"Acquire wisdom! Acquire understanding! Do not forget nor turn away from the words of my mouth."
(Proverbs 4:5 NASB)

"He who restrains his words has knowledge, And he who has a cool spirit is a man of understanding."
(Proverbs 17:27 NASB)

Now, let's explore the three words that the Bible says we need to be wise—wisdom, understanding, and knowledge.

Wisdom. This is the decision to act or speak to produce a "Triple Win": God wins, others win, and we win. To overcome our anger, we must dig for wisdom. The wisest people take a step back before deciding and look for information, connections, and applications they don't know. Wisdom isn't usually the first thing that comes to our mind. Usually, the first thing that comes to mind is what we want most or what would please us. If we use anger to get what we want, we are fools. Wisdom means playing out possible actions until the outcome is good for everybody.

Think to yourself, "If I do what I want, I win, but someone else I care about loses. I will not have found wisdom until everybody wins." God tells us to cry out to Him to give us wisdom we can't see at first. James 1:5 says, "If any of you lacks wisdom, you should ask God, who gives generously to all without finding fault, and it will be given to you." I find that praying for wisdom and receiving an answer can take several hours to a week or two. We need to slow the decision-making process, so we have time to receive back God's wisdom.

"God, how do I handle this situation? It is making me so frustrated and bitter. Show me the wisdom that will give everyone a win." Run tests on how long it takes for God to get back to you with a new idea, a book, a friend who tells you something you need, a Scripture verse, an article, etc. He will answer, so look for it.

Understanding. The Hebrew word for understanding is *binah*, which means discerning or having insight into the connections between decisions, people, and things.[8] If we are going to gain understanding, we must think further into the future and further out into people networks. We must ask, "What will happen if I say this or do that, and how will the other people respond?"

So many times in my life, I have played checkers while life has been playing chess. I played for one move without realizing there would be consequences that could significantly impact me and others. I've often gotten things off my chest, but I didn't understand how spewing my thoughts or opinions would damage the relationship or the workplace for weeks. I can think back on a number of times when I said exactly what I was feeling and destroyed a relationship. Can you relate?

Instead, we must cram understanding into the gap between stimulus and response. Within that gap, ask, "What will happen if I let my anger out?" Think of this just like a good chess player who moves the piece in their mind to the desired place but does not take their hand off of the piece. What are all the moves the opponent could take from this move? If you say this, then what will the other person feel? What will the other person do in reaction? What will you be tempted to do in response to their move? What will they do then? You can save yourself so much grief and brokenness if you practice your conversations and actions beforehand. Understand the possible consequences that could come from your anger. Don't let your anger out if you don't want those bad outcomes.

Knowledge. The Hebrew meaning of the word knowledge (*da'at*) is information and skill.[9] If we had all the pertinent information, we wouldn't get upset. We often get angry because we don't know how to do something, so it seems impossible. We need to learn some new skill or watch a video on how to do the thing we don't know about. It can be helpful to assume that if you are angry or frustrated about something, you are missing some information or skill. Embrace the idea that information and skill pieces may be missing when you feel angry. Calm down and search for what is missing instead of yelling or acting impulsively.

In their fascinating book *Crucial Conversations*,[10] the authors tell us that we all have a path to action that goes through four steps.

Facts —> Stories —> Emotions —> Action

All of us do the same thing. We take a few facts (not all the facts), tell ourselves a story about those few facts, feel emotions (react to) based on the story we have told ourselves, and then act or speak based on those emotions. This means that if we were to add more facts and have a more complete story, our feelings would be different, and we would speak or act entirely differently. Basically, these writers say that if we do what King David told his son Solomon to do—acquire more wisdom, understanding, and knowledge—our lives would be different.

We must spend more time gathering facts to get the complete, real story. There is information that can change our anger into peace. There are consequences of our anger that can stop us before we let our anger out. Some words and actions can reduce or eliminate anger. We just don't know them yet.

SEEKING WISDOM, UNDERSTANDING, AND KNOWLEDGE

- ❑ Where am I tempted to respond too quickly before I have wisdom? What consequences do I need to become aware of?
  - with my spouse
  - with my children
  - at work
  - while driving
  - playing sports
  - in finances

- ❑ How can I search for wisdom, understanding, and knowledge when I feel the first twinges of anger? What new information do I need?
- ❑ Who do I need to talk to who will give me wisdom, understanding, and knowledge about the situation making me angry?
- ❑ What phrases and actions do I need to create a triple win, where God wins, others win, and I win?
- ❑ What resource do I need to consult?
- ❑ What other good options are there?

CALM-DOWN CARD: FIVE STEPS TO WISDOM, UNDERSTANDING, AND KNOWLEDGE

I ran across a helpful illustration to know the difference between wisdom and knowledge that highlights the practical difference: "Knowledge is knowing that tomato is a fruit. Wisdom is not putting the tomato in a fruit salad." To reset your anger, try the following exercises. Make a calm-down card of the five steps below and carry it with you. Next time you get angry, focus on bringing more wisdom, understanding, and knowledge into your life, and watch it change the level of your anger, bitterness, and frustration.

1. Ask God to give you wisdom before you act on the irritating or maddening situation.

2. Ask other people for perspectives on the situation.

3. Think through the next three things that could happen if you do what you want.

4. Ask yourself, others, and God what information you could be missing that would help.

5. What skills do you or others need to make this situation peaceful?

   • Be silent.

   • Ask more questions.

   • No decisions until the emotions are lowered.

   • Take a break from the conversation.

   • Recite James 1:19 or Ephesians 4:26 in your head.

   • Say to the person, "I am flooded right now, and I want to discuss this, but now is not a good time. I will get back to you."

   • Do a workout.

   • Walk away for a little bit of time.

   • Count to ten slowly, or one hundred if you are outraged.

   • Recite Proverbs 4:5: "Get wisdom, get understanding; do not forget my words and turn away from them."

   • Say, "I would love to talk with you about this, but now is not a good time."

   • Recite Proverbs 17:27: "The one who uses knowledge uses words with restraint; and whoever has understanding is even-tempered."

SEEK WISDOM FOR THE TRIPLE WIN

Dear Heavenly Father,

Lord, show me what is wise so that You win, the other person wins, and I win. Who do I need to talk to before I respond? Please show me what resources I need to check with. Show me what other options I need to consider that I am unaware of now. Show me how not to be quick-tempered. Thank You for dying on the cross for my sins. Make me calm on the outside while I seek wisdom on the inside.

In the Name of the Lord Jesus Christ, Amen

D A Y

ADD MORE TIME BETWEEN EVERYTHING

Ecclesiastes 3:1

One wise woman who mentored me and my wife during our parenting years showed us how to expand time and stop being frazzled. She had four young children, but she was never stressed out. She told us that she would estimate how long it would take to get somewhere or accomplish some chore, and then she would add half an hour or an hour to her thinking about that trip or activity. If the kids acted up or needed to be re-instructed, she had the time built in to do it. When we added this extra time element into our travel and parenting, we eliminated a lot of frustration and anger. Add more time, and you will introduce a new level of peace and calm to your life.

Our society is constantly trying to do something in less time than it takes. One of the jobs I had in college was to drive a truck for a major beverage company. I was trained by an expert who was slow and methodical. He was usually the last one out of the yard, but the first one done in the afternoon. He looked over his load in the morning and had the various cases moved around based on what stops he had in which order. He never hurried but just kept going at a very reasonable pace. With all of his pre-work, every stop was easier and quicker. He had thought through his day and how to make it better. His patience and wisdom in the beginning made his whole day go smoother.

God tells us there is a right amount of time for everything. To stay calm and peaceful, we need to give each activity, person, and task the proper amount of time and process.

Notice Ecclesiastes 8:6— "For there is a proper time and procedure for every delight ..." If you are constantly angry, frustrated, or hurried, then maybe you are trying to make things go faster than they really require. We often think we can get more done in a day by going faster. What usually happens is that we are just more upset and prone to anger.

Notice Ecclesiastes 3:1— "There is an appointed time for everything. And there is a time for every event under heaven ..." What is the appointed time to do something without anger or frustration at a level of excellence? Allocate that much time. Stop trying to skimp on activities and people who need more time.

Through the Scriptures, God tries to give us the power and wisdom to live a great life full of love, but we keep asking Him to provide us with the ability to do things faster.

Notice Galatians 5:22–23 and what God gives us— "But the fruit of the Spirit is love, joy, peace, patience, kindness, goodness, faithfulness, gentleness, self-control." Accept God's gift of patience and let things have the time they need to be done well. This strategy for overcoming anger involves giving God, yourself, and others more time.

Colossians 3:12 gives us another secret to a great life: "So, as those who have been chosen of God, holy and beloved, put on a heart of compassion, kindness, humility, gentleness, and **patience**." As God's son or daughter, you can put on qualities He gives you that you don't usually have. Isn't it interesting that God gives us powerful gifts we don't want? We want speed, power, sin without consequences, our way, and fulfilling our desires. Stop and accept the gifts of God's Spirit and let Him make you compassionate and kind, thinking about others and being under control, with lots of time. I am convinced that one of the devil's great ploys to make us sin is to speed us up in all areas of life.

Several years ago, I went through a job change. I could almost always be home in a few minutes at my original job. But the new job required a lot of driving, and I was sometimes eight hours away from home when I finished the day. If I tried to be precise about when I would be home, I would always predict incorrectly and be late because of traffic, gas, people, length of meetings, and so forth. Since I needed to tell my family when I might be home so they could plan their schedule, I often told them when I could be home if everything went perfectly, but that usually didn't work. So, I took the advice of our parenting mentor and applied her "add more time" tactic. I soon discovered a way to always be on time or early by thinking through the worst-case scenario for getting home, and then I added two hours. That way, I would always be home before the guesstimated time. My reward was that I was always cheered for getting home early.

Instead of being stressed out and getting mad because traffic was bad, I had created a foolproof way to be calm and on time or early. Sure, there were a few times when I was right on time because everything that could go wrong went wrong—but I was still on time! I wasn't mad. They weren't mad. Nobody was upset because I had created ample time to accomplish all the meetings and driving. My children still call me an over-estimator, but it removes time pressure from my life, and I don't get angry anymore about being rushed or late because I am always on time.

Adding more time has made me realize that so much of my anger was time-related. I now estimate that I have plenty of time to complete simple tasks. If this sounds like you, don't put yourself under time pressure. Build in plenty of time to accomplish the tasks you need to.

ADDING TIME TO YOUR SCHEDULE

Look at your schedule and decide where you can loosen some time allotments. If your best amount of time to do something is half an hour, schedule ninety minutes. In most cases, you get to say how much time you need for a particular activity. Getting something done without anger is more valuable than getting three things done with anger. How much time do you need to add to normal activities so you can be calm when emergencies crop up? Try a few of these for one to two weeks and see how much your anger lessens.

- ❏ Add one hour to the time needed to get somewhere.
- ❏ Add one hour to the time you allotted for preparation.
- ❏ Add one hour to any activity you engage in.
- ❏ Add a half hour to an hour to every meeting for clean-up, contemplation, and preparation for the next meeting.
- ❏ Add one hour to clean up anything you are involved in.

HELP TO MAKE MORE TIME

Dear Heavenly Father,

I admit I cannot control my anger on my own. Show me how to add enough time to every activity so I won't be angry if things don't go as planned. Help me to see where, when, and how much time I need to add to change from angry to calm and cool. Please come into my life at a new level and save me from my own destructive reactions. I need to see with new eyes and be willing to create enough time to get the job done. Thank You for dying on the cross for my sins. Make me the kind of person You want me to be. I know that this may make me seem odd to those who remember me rushing around to get stuff done at the last minute, but I need to have room so I don't get angry.

In the Name of the Lord Jesus Christ, Amen

"YOU DO NOT HAVE
BECAUSE YOU DO
NOT ASK."

—James 4:3

D A Y

TELL GOD WHAT YOU POSITIVELY WANT IN LIFE

James 4:3

"Until you can state what you want positively, you are not ready to open your mouth."

I remember one leader saying that and I leaned in to listen more. "As an angry person, I was always ready to be negative and point out what was wrong with something or someone and what should change. But we are not really ready to talk about changes until we can say what we want positively." Focusing on the negative must stop as it fuels our anger. We must stop whining to God and others about all the negative and start asking and praying for what we really want in the positive. The apostle James chastises Christians for not using this powerful method for bringing about change: "You do not have because you do not ask" (James 4:3). So it's time to start asking God to help us figure out what we do **want**, not for what we **don't want**.

I want the kids to behave like this … in this situation.

How do we get there?

I want to have this kind of conversation with my spouse.

How do we get there?

I want this kind of job where I have these responsibilities and this pay.

How do I get there?

I want the evenings to look like this.

How do we get there?

I want the mornings to be like this.

How do we get there?

In my journey to reset my anger, I've had to remember that raw anger is destructive. Only processed anger is usable energy. You have to let all the energy inside you begin solving the positive puzzles.

What would the situation look like if it had been done well?

How would the interaction go if it was done right or with peace?

What would I do differently if I wanted a peaceful conversation with my spouse?

What parenting process or system would ensure we don't have the disaster we just had again?

We are so trained to think negatively. It often takes a while before you can think in positive terms, but you can begin to think positively and start making that happen through your words, actions, and prayers. Start thinking about what you want your life to look like in the positive.

It's essential to know that there are nine relational gardens, or arenas, in life: Marriage, Family, Work, Finances, God, Friends,

Church, Society, and Self. We will consistently experience positive outcomes in these areas when we focus on the positive rather than the negative.

Parenting: How do you want the kids to behave? Instead of constantly being upset about their behavior, ask how you want them to interact with you.

Work: What do you want your day to look like? Instead of railing against how many interruptions you have, envision an alternative kind of day.

Marriage: What do you hope your marital interactions will be like? Rather than getting mad with how your spouse is right now, what positive thing do you see?

Finances: What do you want your finances to be like? Aim at a positive financial future instead of getting upset about who overspent or bought the wrong thing.

Until you can state what you want positively, you don't know what you want. This focus on finding the positive goal and process will require a lot of energy. You will get that energy from your processed anger. The negative is easy, but the positive is hard and comes with details and processes. Once you have clearly identified what you positively want (an idea that is a win for everyone), then you can start using your energy to plan how to get there.

It's important to note that when we are under the influence of anger, we want everything instantaneously. But when the energy has been processed, and you're ready to think positively and constructively, you will be prepared to take the time needed to bring about all the changes you want. You'll tap into the gift of patience discussed in the previous strategy and develop a positive plan for your nine relationships.

Years ago, I knew that some of the conversations I wanted to have with my kids would be five years down the road when they were ready. I understood that some changes I wanted at work would take six months to a year. Some of the things I wanted in our marriage would be years in the making. But because I had a plan and a vision for how things could be in the positive, I was willing to wait. My processed anger provided the energy to wait the necessary months and years to see the results.

You are probably already doing this positive long-range planning and dreaming in some areas of your life. For example, think about the whole issue of retirement. If you and your spouse are going to enjoy a great retirement, both of you will have to contribute to an investment plan that is fifteen to thirty years in the future. The same is true with many other things in your life. Any great relationship takes time to build. What type of relationship do you want with your children five years in the future? Describe it positively. What do you want your work life to be like five to ten years in the future? Describe it positively in terms of what you are doing, what you are getting paid, who you are working for, and what level of authority and responsibility you have. Think through the types of interactions and the flow you are going for.

When we offer these positive statements, plans, and dreams to God as prayers, Scripture tells us His energy is connected to our dreams.

Be anxious for nothing but with prayer and supplication let your request be made known to God and the peace of God which surpasses all understanding will guard your hearts and minds in Christ Jesus.
(Philippians 4:6-7)

MAXIMIZING THE NINE RELATIONSHIPS IN YOUR LIFE

God wants us to ask Him **for what we do want, not what we don't want**. I can remember years ago when I started taking this idea seriously. I wrote down what I righteously and positively wanted in each of the nine gardens of life. I then prayed every day that God would allow us (Him and me) to accomplish them. I call these idealization exercises. What do you really want in each arena of life?

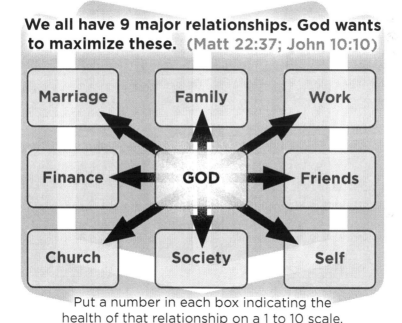

We all have 9 major relationships. God wants to maximize these. (Matt 22:37; John 10:10)

Marriage	Family	Work
Finance	GOD	Friends
Church	Society	Self

Put a number in each box indicating the health of that relationship on a 1 to 10 scale.

At the beginning of every year, I will take the time to write a page or more about what I want in each area of my life within the next five years. I spend a few months thinking and dreaming of the ideal relationship in each area five years from now, based on Jesus's statement in the fourth beatitude: "Blessed are those who hunger and thirst after righteousness, for they shall be satisfied" (Matthew 5:6). God wants me to go after all the righteousness I can in my life, like a person who is starving and even dying of thirst. The righteousness He wants me to go after is in these relational categories.

When I have written down everything I can, I go back through and weed out the selfish ideas. I keep any idea that benefits God's glory, others, and myself. Then, I begin praying about God bringing these into my life. I ask God for what I want, and answers start to come. God shows me how to accomplish my goals. I might read a book that explains how to make huge improvements in some areas. I may get blessed with a person, a gift, or a verse that moves one of the goals much closer to reality. Sometimes, I want a particular answer before God gives me one. I stay patient, keep planning, keep praying, and I usually find that God gives me what I want or something better. My prayer list is my list of what I want in each area of life. "God, this is what I want you to do for me within five years."

Many of you are saying to yourself as you read this, "This is a lot of trouble. I hope this happens to me, but I don't want to write the lists for each relationship. I don't want to pray about these goals and dreams every day." Let me say that you will not get the benefit until you actually do this exercise. You will not see God's power released on your dreams. Tell God what you really want; don't just whine. Pray, pray, pray, and make plans to change the situation if you can. Ask God to show you what and how to change to make the relationship or the situation different.

BUILDING A POSITIVE LIFE

Dear Heavenly Father,

I admit I am angry because what I didn't want to happen has happened again. I want to stop wasting my energy on the negative. I want to build a positive life. Lord, show me what I could have in my life if I hunger and thirst after righteousness. Give me the energy to make the lists and pray about my righteous desires daily until You make them happen in my life. I will give You the glory for all You do. I am so grateful You have not given up on me when others have. You want me to fill my life with love and joy. I want what You want, Lord Jesus; show me how to cooperate with You so I can have the peace, love, relationships, and grace You want me to have.

In Jesus's Name, Amen

"JESUS EXPECTS US TO LOVE OUR ENEMIES AS A WAY TO DEAL WITH THOSE WHO IRRITATE US OR MAKE US ANGRY."

—Gil Stieglitz

D A Y

LOVE MORE

Luke 6:27-37

In the famous passage in Luke 6, Jesus gives us the antidote to anger: we do what Jesus says to do, and things will change drastically in our lives. This difficult yet practical advice deals with those who get in our way or are against us for some reason. What Jesus tells us to do is not what you'd think—it all comes down to loving more. Take a look.

> But I say to you who hear, *love* your enemies, *do good* to those who hate you, *bless* those who curse you, *pray* for those who mistreat you. Whoever hits you on the cheek, offer him the other also; and whoever takes away your coat, do not withhold your shirt from him either. *Give* to everyone who asks of you, and whoever takes away what is yours, do not demand it back. Treat others the same way you want them to treat you. If you love those who love you, what credit is that to you? For even sinners love those who love them. If you do good to those who do good to you, what credit is that to you? For even sinners do the same. If you lend to those from whom you expect to receive, what credit is that to you? Even sinners lend to sinners in order to receive back the same

amount. *But love your enemies, and do good, and lend, expecting nothing in return;* and your reward will be great, and you will be sons of the Most High; for He Himself is kind to ungrateful and evil men. Be merciful, just as your Father is merciful. (Luke 6:27–37 NASB, emphases mine)

These are Jesus's statements about overcoming anger, and I know what you're thinking: "This is so over the top!" We're used to seeing this as "religious" language, but surely Jesus doesn't expect us to really do these things, does He? But yes, Jesus expects us to love our enemies as a strategy for dealing with those who irritate us or make us angry. To love someone well means to meet their needs, pursue them, or please them somehow. He essentially says, "Refuse to respond negatively—go the positive route instead." He knows we won't get over the anger until we go beyond the normal.

God's Word says we should do good to those who oppose or anger us. We can defuse our anger by thinking of positive benefits we can add to the other person. We bless people who are slandering us rather than curse them, meaning we identify what they are doing well and let them know we see these benefits and talk about them. When people are mistreating us, we should pray for them rather than pray and plot against them. We are to turn the other cheek to be slapped rather than bash their heads in like we might want to do. Jesus also tells us we should give to people rather than withhold from them. We will trust God to make up for the difficulties these people cause us and others. Our efforts will promote peace rather than strife as we show mercy to people who have not been merciful to us. These strategies are real and work to change our circumstances, defuse a situation, and repair relationships.

By practicing these loving-more strategies, we can increase the gap between stimulus and response. Jesus knows this and tells us how to respond in a non-angry way—in a peaceful and relationship-building way. It is very counter-intuitive. Years ago, I worked for a soft drink company, driving trucks for them to earn my way through graduate school. I had just started and had a great trainer who was teaching me the ropes about how to do the job. I was hired before the

Fourth of July weekend, and the company was short on drivers for all the orders. To get more products out, they had all of us new drivers (like me) start delivering products before we were fully trained. They brought supervisors out of the office buildings to be with us.

My supervisor was a very angry, cantankerous man who I will call Ralph. Ralph jumped in my truck and started swearing at me almost immediately. I didn't know what I was doing, and he pointed out everything I did wrong ... everything. He swore at me for eight to ten hours every day for a week. I heard swear words I didn't know were swear words. He never did any of the actual work; he was just bossing me around. It got so bad that the store owners would say to me, "Hang in there, kid. He will get his someday." On several occasions, I asked the Lord, "Can I just not be a Christian for a few minutes? I will fix this problem." Of course, the Lord never said yes. I just had to take it. "Faster," "Faster, you blankety-blank idiot." "Don't do it that way, blankety-blank, stupid." "How come you blank didn't do this." "How come you blankety-blank did that?"

Finally, the rush was over a week after the holiday, and I was sent back to my trainer to finish my training. It was a huge relief. After the first day back, my trainer asked, "You're done! You are faster than most of the drivers here." I realized that the hell week I spent with Ralph had trained me to be better and faster than most of the other drivers. God had worked through Ralph to make this hard job easy. In a very intense way, God used Ralph to humble me and train me in a very short period of time.

One day, God prompted me to do what Jesus said we are to do with our enemies—"Bless those who curse you." I didn't really want to, but I found Ralph's office and asked if I could talk with him for a minute. "Sure," he said. I took a deep breath and said, "I wanted to thank you for all of your training. David (my trainer) tells me I am one of the fastest and best drivers in the yard now. Your being hard on me has improved me significantly. Thank you." He thanked me for saying that, and from that day forward, Ralph, who cussed and swore at everybody, never swore at me again. I had blessed him when he had cursed me, and it changed him.

I've seen firsthand how the antidote to anger is love and joy. I naturally would think that revenge, resentment, and payback would be the way to diminish my anger at an unfair situation. But God showed me that blessing Ralph was a better way to change the situation than expressing my anger or ingratitude. God's ways are not man's ways, but they do work. I have needed to use these techniques on many occasions to overcome my anger at people who have betrayed me, girlfriends who rejected me, organizations who have cheated me, and leaders who have lied to me. The way to overcome injustice is not revenge but more love and joy. The answer is not bitterness but gratitude and a positive focus.

My journey to reset my anger required that I see what God was doing from a much bigger perspective. I have had to become much more loving and joyful to those who once made me so mad. Doing so overwhelms my natural self-focus and irritation at people, and in the end, we are no longer enemies.

I can remember one time when I was upset at my wife for something. Now, please realize that my wife is only wrong once every six years. I am wrong weekly, if not daily. She is practically perfect in every way. So, this was the second time in our marriage she had been wrong, and I was excited because she would have to apologize to me for once. I got really excited about this. Then I made the mistake of praying about it, and I heard God say, "Forgive her, let it go."

What? I did not want to hear that, so I argued with God. I had been waiting for six years for this, and she really was wrong. If I didn't call her on it, it would be another six years before she did anything wrong. Well, God and I went round and round about this for a while, and I lost the argument. Then God added, "I want you to go to town and get her a gift to thank her for all the stuff she does for you and the girls." We had another discussion about that ... it seemed unreasonable. But I eventually packed up the kids, and we went to the department store to get Mommy a gift to say thank you for being such a great mommy. The kids were all excited.

We ended up getting her a new bathrobe and some new slippers. The store wrapped them up, and the girls were so excited about giving Mommy her gift. By the time she came home (she was doing her master's work in nursing that day), we were all excited about thanking her for the great person she was and how she made our lives so good. She received the gift and broke down in tears as she got hugs from the girls and me. Later, she apologized for what she had done in a much deeper way than I expected. I so much wanted to nail her for what she did, but God turned a negative thing into a positive thing—a peaceful thing. This exemplifies Jesus's practical way of defusing a difficult conversation into something healing. Seeing how His way worked was amazing, even though I was reluctant to try it.

ANTIDOTES TO ANGER

Below is a list of loving actions that God may ask you to do to those who anger you. Is He asking you to do any of these toward your spouse, family, colleagues or bosses, banker or lender, God, friends, church folks, neighbors, community people, politicians, or yourself? If you throw yourself into doing these positive things for your enemies, I think you will notice how your anger dissipates; it will change your perspective and dissolve anger. Write these things down on a 3" x 5" card and carry it with you. Ask God which loving action you should do for the ones who make you upset or oppose you.

1. Love: meet a need, pursue them, please them

2. Do good: benefit them in some way

3. Bless: say how they have benefitted you

4. Pray: pray for them rather than against them

5. Turn the other cheek: go beyond what is required concerning them

6. Give: share, loan, and help those who ask

7. Treat others as you want to be treated. If the situation were reversed, how would you want to be treated?

Yes, I know you want to tell me you can't do these things for your enemies, and you are right. But listen for the whispers of the Holy Spirit as to which of these you should do and move forward in faith. God will provide you with the power to do these things that you don't feel like doing. Your anger will be eliminated by doing these positives in God's power.

BLESSING MY ENEMY

Dear Heavenly Father,

I admit I want to unleash on _____. I need you to be in me, with me, over me, and through me. Give me the energy and ability to go beyond what is normal and bless them somehow to defuse my anger at them. Show me what aspect of love will make this situation good for everyone. I need Your love because I am mad at them, and right now, I don't have any love for them. Empower me to go the second mile. Thank You for dying on the cross for my sins. Give me the love and joy I do not have in myself.

In Jesus's Name, Amen

"SURRENDER THE
RIGHT TO WIN TO KEEP
FROM GETTING ANGRY
WHEN YOU LOSE."

—Gil Stieglitz

D A Y

SURRENDER THE RIGHT TO WIN

Romans 6:11; Proverbs 12:16

Many people who are regularly angry are often very competitive. They want to win at everything. Their idea of fun is winning; if they are not winning, they are not having fun.

I can remember when one highly professional person with a distinguished career and multiple impressive degrees was over at our house with some other couples. We decided to play a trivia game. It was going well until this individual started losing. He couldn't handle it and eventually got up from the table in a huff and walked into the other room. He was really hot under the collar because he hated losing. He was clearly the smartest person in the room, but the game did not show how smart he was, and this made him mad. Some other people had gotten the correct answer, and he couldn't take it. This guy was so used to winning that he had not developed a good meekness response whenever he was not winning. He liked being the smartest, fastest, most strategic person in the room, but in this game, he wasn't. Eventually, he stayed in the next room while we finished the game. Then we just talked in general so we wouldn't trigger that response in him again. He was a great winner but a sore loser.

If you battle with being a sore loser, you can certainly relate to this story. But if you are serious about getting control of your anger, you need to figure out a way not to let losing make you angry. One of the ways you can do that is to surrender the right to win before you begin an activity. This strategy is another stimulus-response gap extender that prevents anger before it gets started. When you know you are usually too quick to respond in a given situation or activity, then surrender your right to win ahead of time.

Let's look at what Scripture says in connection with this idea:

"Even so consider yourselves to be dead to sin, but alive to God in Christ Jesus."
(Romans 6:11)

To apply this verse to your anger problem, decide ahead of time to die to your "right" to win. The key is to be alive to the voice of God in your life and tone down the voice of "I should win!" When I was battling my anger issues and started putting this exercise into practice, I discovered there was a bigger objective than winning when I played chess with my kids. Instead of needing to win, I started delighting in teaching them the game, giving them confidence, and developing someone who wanted to play it. It was up to me to die to my "right" to win, and it paid dividends.

"A fool's anger is known at once,
But a prudent man conceals dishonor."
(Proverbs 12:16)

Too many of us plan out all kinds of things, like how we will get from point A to point B, what we must have to enjoy a vacation, and how much we must save and invest to retire comfortably. Likewise, we can plan how to avoid being angry and spoiling a great time. This verse is saying that the prudent person is the one who plans and thinks through what will happen and how to avoid the dangers. Our anger is a danger to many people's good times. Plan to surrender the right to win before you get into the situations where this temptation usually comes up.So many times, we get angry about the same things over and over. The kids, the boss, the sports team, the finances, the marriage, the politics, etc. We have defined what winning looks like in these areas, and when that is not happening, we are unhappy. Surrender your right to win because, in many cases, you will not win. Just like every sports fan, I have favorite teams that don't win. I have had to adjust to the fact that it is great if my teams win, but it is not the end of the world if they don't. I need to applaud the teams that win this year and hope my teams win next year. But if you demand or expect your teams to win each year, you are not living in reality and are likely angry a lot.

When I began learning how to create a gap between the stimulus to anger and my response, I had to deal with my involvement with sports. I liked to win. No matter what sport I was playing, I should win. But that had caused me, on many occasions, to lose my temper. Christ still had a lot of work to do on me to separate me from a destructive engagement of my anger. It showed up whenever I got competitive.

Finally, I discovered that if I got down on the side of the court and surrendered my right to win before I played, I was a lot better. I would play for the exercise. I would play for the fun. I would play for the teamwork. I would play to express my skills. I would play for the practice. But I would not play for the sole purpose of winning. This was brought home to me once when a group of us were invited to play one of the best collegiate basketball teams in the region in a fundraiser for the college. We went into the contest thinking we could win, but we quickly discovered we were no match for these incredibly tuned and skilled players. We were going to lose, but we could have a lot of fun playing. And we did. There was a different point to the game than just winning.

Here are some other areas where I had to surrender my right to win:

- I had to surrender my right to have the kids in perfect control during our parenting process. I could do everything right, but it would still be messy. They were learning, and so was I.

- I had to surrender the expectation for my wife to read my mind. I actually needed to communicate with her using words, letters, texts, phone calls, etc., sometimes multiple times.

- I had to stop believing that God desired to do everything I wanted to have done. I had to adjust to His will. He is always working on a more important agenda than what I want.

- I had to surrender the right to go at whatever speed I wanted to go … in whatever lane I tried to drive in. Other people on the road also have rights. I am not the king of the freeway whenever I get on it. Everyone else is not an idiot just because they are not driving like me or making way for me.

- I had to give up the right to play basketball because it made me angry on a regular basis. This was the cut-your-right-hand-off tactic but also a level of surrendering the right to win. There have been many bad boys in the NBA. Two of these villains had a reputation for their superior skills and their anger and willingness to do almost anything to get their teams to win. Rasheed Wallace and Draymond Green. Both of them in their era took their desire to win too far and were disciplined repeatedly by the league. They were great basketball players willing to do way too much to get the win they craved.

In your effort to surrender the right to win, think ahead and pre-plan what you must do to avoid anger. Stop wanting to always be in charge. Surrender your right to be in control. When you surrender your right to be right before you get started, you will find a new ability to stay calm in the various situations where you are usually volatile.

SURRENDERING YOUR RIGHT TO WIN

1. Kneel down and surrender the right to win before you get home, go into the office, play your sport, or see your kids and have to parent them. Tell God that you realize He may have a bigger objective than you winning or getting your way. Tell Him that you surrender your right to win, to be right, and always to get your way.

2. Decide what the objective can be rather than winning. What is God's objective for your situation?

   - Peace, where everyone is calm and under control.
   - Relational, where the relationship can get deeper and more enjoyable.
   - Emotional, where people have the right to be emotional in safety.
   - Physical, where everyone has a feeling of safety and freedom from violence.
   - Spiritual, where God is acknowledged and His presence is felt.
   - Mental, where multiple points of view are discussed and understood.

3. Refuse to use your old means to get your way.

   - Disagreeing with your spouse to confuse her even though you know she is right.
   - Using tears, anger, or yelling to derail a discussion because you are losing.
   - Do not try to be louder and bigger than your kids to prevent them from expressing what they think or feel. Instead, listen to your kids and hear what they are saying rather than just trying to have them listen and obey you.

4. Surrender the right to use any means to win or remain in control. There will be all kinds of tactics, distractions, and

objections that will come to your mind to keep the other person from winning, such as:

- Picking a fight rather than letting their train of thought be accepted.
- Walking away because they are winning.
- Disagreeing with them even though you know they are right.
- Pointing out something they did wrong that is disconnected from the discussion so they don't win this discussion.
- Being loud or belligerent.
- Making statements like, "You don't know what you are saying," or "But you said ..."
- Picking apart some random detail rather than dealing with the real issue.
- Interrupting the discussion and having the other person do something you know they will do just to prove you are in charge.

SURRENDERING MY RIGHT TO WIN

Dear Heavenly Father,

I admit, Lord, that I have used violence and/or the threat of violence to get my way. That is wrong. I admit that I have lied or cheated to get my own way. I have used all kinds of distractions and other means so I wouldn't lose an argument. That is wrong. Right now, I surrender my right to win, be right, and be in control. I want the peace of God and good relationships to surround me. Help me to stop playing "King of the Hill." Show me how to fill my life with loving relationships.

In Jesus's Name, Amen

"WE CAN LEARN FROM THE PAST TO AVOID FUTURE MISTAKES."

—Gil Stieglitz

D A Y

USE A TIME MACHINE

Proverbs 19:11

Imagine sitting in a time machine, and you could move forward a hundred years into the future or back to any other time. I know this concept is science fiction, but we can apply it to the anger reset. What if you could go back in time and change something that went wrong in the past so that it wouldn't happen again? Like a situation that leads to unleashing your explosive anger and causing a break in a relationship with someone you love. Or an event where your toxic words spilled all over someone important to you.

While in reality, we can't change the past, we can learn from it to avoid making mistakes in the future, and that is what this next anger-reset strategy is about. I want you to revisit the past in your mind to learn what you can do in the future to prevent anger from occurring.

Hopefully, by this point, you will be much better at separating the stimulus for your anger from the response to it. However, at some point in the reset process, you will have to start working on anger before it begins. I'm happy to tell you that learning how to stop the feelings before they begin is possible.

Look at what Scripture says about planning and looking back to bring about changes in the future.

"A man's discretion makes him slow to anger,
And it is his glory to overlook a transgression."
(Proverbs 19:11)

The word *discretion* carries a connotation of planning and a plan. We all need to make a plan so that the worst of our emotional reactions don't jump out. When you have a plan to avoid your anger, you can be a person who is slow to anger.

If you mentally and emotionally work through what you can say or do before the situation reveals your anger, then you can change a few things and not trigger the anger at all. Now, I know that you want the other person to change—that would be the thing to eliminate the anger—but that is often an unrealistic expectation you have no control over. But you can control what you say and do to eliminate the anger from even appearing next time.

We can imagine what would happen if we said or did something. We are in a time machine, traveling to the future and seeing the reactions and results of our words and actions. We play out what will happen in our minds. If it causes us to get angry at some point, we will think of a different way of saying or doing it.

Husbands and wives can spend five to ten minutes making sure they communicate without an attitude. Many people are more accurate than they realize if they apply past reactions to possible future conversations.

Employees and employers can use a time machine to go back and study the patterns in the company. They use this data to change a few things about their work, their interactions, and their work life so that it eliminates anger. Often, the difference between a good meeting and a disaster is a few transitional statements or different actions or proposals.

Parents can change their schedules or their kids' schedules to eliminate some of the whining and resistance. By thinking ahead, parents realize they need much more time to get stuff done if they want to parent without anger. They fly back into their mental time machine and realize they will have to give more of themselves to their children to overcome their anger and have a great family.

I can remember when we had a dog and a cat as pets in our house for the kids. The cat pestered the dog, and the dog barked and growled at the cat. It was driving me nuts. I remember getting in my mental DeLorean and punching in the time before the last fight between the dog and the cat. I thought through what could be different so this would stop happening. What would eliminate their fight so it would eliminate my anger? How could I turn my unrealistic expectation that they wouldn't fight into a realistic one?

I remember in one of their last fights, the cat was on the couch and scratched the dog as she went by right beneath her. The dog chased the cat all around the house, with the cat having no place to really hide. I realized that if the cat and dog were separated by more space, they would not be as prone to bark, claw, and fight. So, I went to a local pet store and bought a cat climbing structure the dog could not use. This meant that the cat could retreat and survey her whole domain but not be able to claw or hiss at the dog. The dog could not go up into the cat structure and would be separated from the cat. It worked beautifully! I eliminated my anger by solving the problem of the dog and the cat fighting.

One man I knew would regularly get angry about misplacing his glasses and being unable to find them when he wanted to read. He thought through this regular occurrence and purchased a little pouch that would hold his glasses near his reading chair. He set up a routine so that he always put the glasses in the pouch and always knew where they would be. This solved his anger over the misplaced glasses.

I used to get angry when the kids did not remember how to behave in a store, restaurant, or grandma's house. I realized they needed to be calmly re-educated and re-trained each time before we went to one of those places. I needed to include a re-education and re-training time before entering the store, entering the restaurant, and going to grandma's. I stopped all the kids before entering the store and told them, "Here is what I expect of you …" "Here are the three to five things I want you to focus on while we are in the store." It is amazing that they did so well with a bit of extra training, and I didn't get angry.

Here are some typical discoveries you might find in your time machine. See if you agree.

- More communication would have changed things.

- More time would have changed things.

- More kindness would have changed things.

- More planning would have changed things.

- More systems and routines would have changed things.

- More education and retraining would have changed things.

- More alignment of goals, ideas, and strategies would have changed things.

These changes are often small, but they make a huge difference. You are cleansing your life of things that trigger anger as much as possible. The wise man or woman stops expecting a different result from the same ingredients. Change what needs to be changed, even if it is small, so that anger can be avoided.

FIRING UP YOUR TIME MACHINE

If you are regularly angry over the same thing, you can change something before it happens the next time. There are always a few things that can change. I call this strategy "Use a Time Machine." You get in your mental DeLorean, fire up the flux capacitor, and go back to before you got angry. Close your eyes and think back for a minute to the last time your anger got away from you ...

1. **What is happening?**

   - Is it the kids who exposed your unrealistic expectations?
   - Is it your lack of time that exposed your unrealistic expectations?
   - Is it your boss who exposed your unrealistic expectations?
   - Is it your spouse who exposed your unrealistic expectations?
   - What is happening that is about to trigger you?

2. **Write it down ...**

   - This happened ...
   - Then that happened ...
   - Then they did this ...
   - Then I got angry, and the whole issue became about my anger instead of the real issue.

3. **Now, what could you have done in time (15 min, 30 min, 1 hour) before this incident that would have eliminated the anger completely?**

   - Could you have reminded the kids what you expected?
   - Could you have left an hour earlier so you would have plenty of time?
   - Could you have finished the boss's project before the meeting?
   - Could you have rephrased your question to your spouse or did what they asked?

4. What 3–5 things could you do that would eliminate the anger from popping up? (Remember, you can't change the past, but you can change what you do in the future.)

-
-
-
-
-

WHAT CAN I CHANGE?

Dear Heavenly Father,

I keep getting angry over this issue, this person, or this situation. I need You to be in me, with me, over me, and through me. Show me how to go back before I get angry and change something(s) so I do not get angry. Thank You for dying on the cross for my sins. Enter into me and allow me to be calm even when I am feeling angry on the inside. What needs to be different next time so this is avoided?

In Jesus's Name, Amen

"OVERCOME YOUR NATURAL POWER TO GO BEYOND ANGER BY USING YOUR ENERGY TO DRAW PEOPLE OUT AND LIFT THEM UP."

—Gil Stieglitz

D A Y

OVERCOME YOUR NATURAL POWER

Philippians 2:3-4

In the wonderful story by Charles Dickens, A Christmas Carol, Ebenezer Scrooge becomes a different person after he is visited by the ghost of his former business partner and the ghosts of Christmas past, present, and future. Scrooge realized from these visits that his anger, greed, and selfishness created a horrible life and future. He changed his mind and admitted that he was on the wrong track in life. With God's help, he knew he had to overcome who he was naturally. He was overbearing and unwilling to see the real people around him. He needed to stop paying attention to the promptings of greed, anger, and power and start listening to the impulses of love, generosity, kindness, and patience.

This transformation over our natural selves is crucial to overcoming anger. We are not just trying to control our anger; we are seeking to allow new impulses to flow through us instead. We may not have visits from the ghosts of the past or future, but we can undergo the same transformation as Scrooge did, from a shriveled life to a life full of love and joy.

Angry people project power through their anger. They can get their way just because people don't want to experience their wrath. Their steamroller approach to getting what they want seriously damages relationships, plus they don't get the genuine ideas of the people around them or the full energy of the people they oppress. True friends work hard to draw out the ideas and dreams of those around them. Angry people often stifle others in ways they don't realize. They are just living their self-focused life. This next strategy will help you overcome your natural power beyond anger and start using your energy to draw people out and lift them up.

The Bible tells us there is a huge blessing if we get beyond our self-focus. If we start treating others with the dignity and respect they deserve, our lives will be richer and better than if we just run over people with our personalities, anger, dreams, and wants.

Do nothing from selfishness or empty conceit, but with humility of mind regard one another as more important than yourselves; do not merely look out for your own personal interests, but also for the interests of others.
(Philippians 2:3-4 NASB)

We must realize that our personality, energy, gender, privileges, and family of origin give us incredible power. We must work hard to draw others out and not walk over them. We must go beyond not being angry. We must become champions of other people by working hard not to control people but to invite them into cooperation and alignment. Draw the other person out and up, and you will gain their wisdom and relationship.

I have had many bosses over my lifetime. Dave was a middle manager at a large company where I worked for a while. He greatly impacted my life because he always looked out for me. He used what little power he had in the company to get me good shifts, good assignments, and extra opportunities. He protected me when bosses above me wanted to throw me under the bus. He helped me in every way he could within the rules of the company. If I messed up, he would tell me, but I knew he was for me. He was not about himself and what he could get out of me; he cared about how I could be a better person and employee. He was someone going to bat for me. I watched him use his personality, position, and influence on me. It made a real difference in my life. I talked with him a few years ago and thanked him for all he had done for me. He thanked me but shrugged it off because it was what he did for everybody. That's how you want people to know you: someone who naturally cares and lifts others up.

Joe Polish has written a terrific book about dealing with people called *What's in It for Them?* This must be our mindset if we are to go beyond anger consistently. We must begin to ask and answer this question to have a different life than the one built by anger.[11] If the other people in our life don't win, then something is wrong. Ask yourself, "What can I do that will truly bless other people?" When we genuinely begin to ask and answer this question, anger will stop being a problem. We will be unleashed to make a huge impact in the lives of the people around us.

The New Testament provides a helpful insight that we are to be pointed toward our neighbor to love them, not the whole world (Matthew 22:39). It is easy to say we want to love the world, but if we cast our net to include "the world," then it's hard to love the real people who are actually in our lives. The great philosopher Voltaire wrote about ways to love the world, but he put up every one of his children for adoption because he didn't want to be bothered.[12] I have found that our culture wants to change the world instead of focusing our love and impact on the people we actually know.

Think about the people you come in contact with each week and how you can make a positive difference in their lives. Use your natural energy and power to bless, encourage, appreciate, and help them. Your life and theirs will change for the better.

USE YOUR ENERGY TO LIFT OTHERS UP

Think about the people in your life, those you regularly deal with in your life, and write their names in the space provided.

- Family members
- Work colleagues
- Neighbors
- Community and church friends
- Hobby/group friends

What would bless the individuals you listed? Ask God to focus you on 1-2 individuals per week and what He wants you to do for them, then follow through with those ideas. Write them down here.

_____

_____

When you interact with someone, ask questions that allow them to explore their ideas.

- Tell me what you (the other person) are thinking.
- How would you (the other person) do this?
- What can we do?
- How can we align our expectations for this trip, this weekend, this bonus, or this new assignment?
- What do you want to accomplish in the next month, 3 months, 6 months, 12 months?

Consider asking someone in your life to join you on a project or giving them a project and letting them run it. Then, they can share the results with you. What can your kids work on with your supervision or partnership? What coworker would benefit from learning from you? Is there a neighbor who needs your help?

_____

_____

Ask the people in your life how you can pray for them, and do this regularly.

DRAWING OTHERS OUT

Dear Heavenly Father,

I realize, Lord, that my personality, gender, privileges, and family of origin give me incredible power. Show me how to draw others out and not walk over them. Lord, help me listen to their ideas, opinions, and plans. Work hard in me to not control people but invite them into cooperation and alignment. I don't want to miss their wisdom and this relationship.

In Jesus's Name, Amen

"WHAT WOULD GOD DO IF YOU GAVE HIM FREE REIN TO STOP YOUR ANGER?"

—Gil Stieglitz

DAY

UNLEASH GOD TO STOP YOUR ANGER

Psalm 4:4; 1 Corinthians 10:13; Philippians 4:6

Diane struggled with saying too much and spewing her anger at those who disagreed with her. She thought maybe God could do something that would block her from saying too much or forcing her opinions on other people, so she asked Him to shut her mouth and not let her talk when she was about to say something she shouldn't. And God did exactly that! When I asked her to describe what it was like, she said it felt like she couldn't talk. Rather than power up and go over God's help, she cooperated with God's block and didn't say a word. When we cry out to God to change something about our lives, He will respond and get us the help we need directly or indirectly (Matthew 7:7).

What do you think God might do if you gave Him free rein to stop you from being angry? God is alive and willing to be active in your life if you ask and cooperate with what He is doing. Now, this strategy is not a substitute for all the other things you are using to move forward in your life of control, peace, and calm—it's a strategy that works in addition to all of that. God tells us He will help us with our anger in the following Scriptures. Let's see how.

1. **He provides escape routes:**

   "No temptation has overtaken you but such as is common to man and with the temptation He will provide a way of escape so you may be able to endure it."
   (1 Corinthians 10:13)

   What escape routes has He given you in the past to keep you from being angry?

2. **He allows us to make requests to help us with anger and anxiety about situations:**

   "Be anxious for nothing but with prayer and supplication let your requests be made known to God and the peace of God will guard your hearts and minds in Christ Jesus."
   (Philippians 4:6)

   What do you want to happen in the event or meeting you are about to have?

3. He knows we will get angry, but there is a way to be angry and not sin:

   "Tremble, and do not sin. Meditate in your heart upon your bed, and be still."
   (Psalm 4:4)

   "Be angry but do not sin."
   (Ephesians 4:26)

   When have you been so upset that you shook or needed to walk away to contain your rage?

God wants us to control our anger because He knows the damage raw anger causes. However, as this next story shows, apologizing isn't always enough to repair the damage.

NAILS IN THE FENCE

There once was a little boy who had a bad temper. His father gave him a bag of nails and told him that every time he lost his temper, he must hammer a nail into the back of the fence.

On the first day, the boy drove thirty-seven nails into the fence. Over the next few weeks, as he learned to control his anger, the number of nails hammered daily gradually dwindled. He discovered holding his temper was easier than driving those nails into the fence.

Finally, the day came when the boy didn't lose his temper at all. He told his father about it, and the father suggested that the boy now pull out one nail for each day he could hold his temper. The days passed, and the young boy was finally able to tell his father that all the nails were gone.

The father took his son by the hand and led him to the fence. He said, "You have done well, my son, but look at the holes in the fence. The fence will never be the same. When you say things in anger, they leave a scar just like this one. You can put a knife in a man and draw it out. It won't matter how often you say I'm sorry; the wound is still there."

The little boy then understood how powerful his words were. He looked up at his father and said, "I hope you can forgive me, Father, for the holes I put in you."

"Of course I can," said the father.[13]

Thankfully, God's mercy will always be available when we express heartfelt regret over our actions. He forgave us once and for all by dying on the cross and taking our penalty upon Himself. He now wants to partner with us to overcome our anger.

WHAT NEW THINGS WILL GOD DO TO HELP YOU CONTROL YOUR ANGER?

Begin this exercise by asking God to do new things to help you control your anger. Also, ask Him for eyes to see what He is already doing to help you manage the expression of your frustration.

1. How has God been trying to divert you from releasing your anger on other people?

   _____

   _____

   _____

2. How can you cooperate with God's way of enduring the pressures and difficulties that trigger your anger?

   _____

   _____

   _____

3. Keep track of what God is doing to interrupt your anger, stop your anger, change the situation, or whatever else He does. When you ask God to intervene, He will. You have to be ready to cooperate with Him. List some things you might be noticing.

   _____

   _____

   _____

UNLEASHING GOD TO CONTROL MY ANGER

Heavenly Father,

Lord, I don't know how to stop being angry. Please give me twenty ways not to be angry next time. Please give me the power to choose a different path next time. I ask that You give me a way to repair the damage I have done through my anger. Give me Your mercy that less damage will happen than should have happened because of what I said or did. Thank You, Lord, for not giving up on me. Keep working inside me. Empower me to be calm and wise as I live before You.

In the Name of the Lord Jesus Christ, Amen

"WE NEED NEW, POSITIVE BRAIN PATHWAYS TO HEAL OUR ANGER."

—Gil Stieglitz

D A Y

18

ASK GOD FOR NOISE-CANCELLING THOUGHTS

Philippians 4:8

Anyone who struggles with a habitual or addictive problem has a noise problem. They hear all the promptings, suggestions, commands, and temptations of their destructive solution. This is called the "noise," which, in this book for anger addiction, is a selfish noise that demands that we get what we want.

As anger addicts, we have become very sensitized to when we are not happy. We receive prompts to be upset about the smallest things, like the kids not minding, the way someone drives, the tone of someone's voice, the lack of a parking spot, etc. Many people realize this is "just the way the world works sometimes," but not us. We are irritated that the world is not how we want it, and we take everything like a personal affront. The noise tells us to explode, take it personally, and lash out with words and wrath. Our expectations are growing and have become obvious on the surface. To deal with this problem, we need to lower the noise. It would be easier to manage our anger if we didn't feel the selfish promptings as much.

Some people have been trained to be irritated by their upbringing. They have been encouraged to be self-focused and not do or think anything they don't find interesting or pleasing. To overcome anger, we have to create different noises in our heads so we do not hear the bitter noises. There are several ways we can potentially lower the noise:

1. Eliminate the things and people who irritate you.

2. Slow down the connection between the prompt to anger and your response.

3. Calm the noise by taking a different lesson from the noise (like engaging in a positive, constructive difference; see Ephesians 4:28).

4. Add more Scripture into your mind to cancel out the noise of the anger.

5. Add more worship songs and positive music to your life.

6. Add more positive thoughts, ideas, plans, memories, and songs to drown out the noise.

7. Add more routines and systems that do not allow you to ignore the anger noise.

The apostle Paul tells us that to live the Christian life, we must force our minds to dwell on good things, even if it is not easy.

Finally, brethren, whatever is true, whatever is honorable, whatever is right, whatever is pure, whatever is lovely, whatever is of good repute, if there is any excellence and if anything worthy of praise, dwell on these things.

(Philippians 4:8)

Science tells us that new neural pathways form when we think new thoughts.[14] New axions reach out and make new connections in our brains whenever we learn something new or train ourselves to think differently. Since anger issues reinforce destructive patterns in our brains, we must create new, positive pathways to heal from anger. We need some new options, and yes, it will take some difficult mental work. Begin by asking yourself questions like the ones below and journal your answers.

- What are my positive thoughts about the future?
- What are my positive ideas about each relational garden in my life?*
- What are my positive plans for the next twelve months?
- What positive memories in each relational garden can I think about rather than let anger fester?

(* Remember from Day 12 that the nine relational gardens are God, Self, Spouse, Family, Work, Church, Community, Finances, and Society.)

I know this is hard mental and emotional work, but God wants to strengthen you to do this work so you are not a slave to your anger. The more you look for the positive things in life, the more you will find. Yes, social media news feeds and videos emphasize the negative because they capture people's attention quicker, but there is good out there all over your life. You must find it. Look for new ways of noticing the awe and inspiration in your everyday life.

Also, don't dismiss the good that is happening to others. We often can become so self-focused that we only want to celebrate the good that happens to us. Create positive "noise" to cancel out the noises of anger and irritability that take up too much space in your brain.

ADDING GOD'S THOUGHTS TO OUR MINDS THROUGH SCRIPTURE

The ancient exercise of biblical meditation is designed to help with this problem of too much noise. It replaces angry, puffed-up noise with God's voice. Biblical meditation requires you to do all kinds of mental and physical actions to repeat Scripture.[15] You could memorize it, study it, confess it, personalize it, draw it, diagram it, act it out, sing it, journal it, or visualize it. If we add more of God's thoughts to our minds, it is easier to hear from Him. Anger and selfishness will win if you do not add pure, positive thoughts to your brain.

We will find what we seek out. You will find things that irritate you if you are looking for things that irritate you. If you are looking for positive things, you will find them. So, if our goal is to fill our minds with positive, constructive thoughts, we will find it when we fill our minds with Scripture. It's like installing noise-cancelling headphones in your head.

Let's get practical about how to do this. The early church taught people to memorize five Scripture passages and repeat them daily.

1. The Great Commandments (Matthew 22:35-40)

2. The Ten Commandments (Exodus 20:1-17)

3. The Lord's Prayer (Matthew 6:9-13)

4. The Beatitudes (Matthew 5:1-12)

5. The Fruit of the Spirit (Galatians 5:22-23)

It may seem like a lot to memorize, but you'll be surprised if you just begin with one and move on to the next one. Memorize these and say them daily as you stand in the shower, stretch, or wait for a meeting. These five passages must become constant sources of positive noise in your head. Many have added the Twenty-third Psalm, the Apostles Creed, Psalm 1, John 15, and others. These Scriptures have words of life and will guide you in the various difficulties and problems you face.

Another biblical meditation technique I use is asking God to show me what I need to know about tomorrow to respond to Him. I look in the Proverbs and Psalms for the day about my issues. God always highlights a passage that stands out for me to focus on. I study and then memorize that verse and say it to myself as I go to sleep. This adds to the "noise" of these verses and God's truths for me tomorrow. In these ways, I drown out the anger and self-focused "noise."

FILLING YOUR MIND WITH POSITIVE MUSIC

God's command is to fill our minds with positive, loving, excellent, and uplifting things (Philippians 4:8). We can do this by listening to more worship music that exalts God and praises Him for what He has done for us. This is more noise-cancelling software, so you don't hear all the promptings to be irritated and mad. Let God speak to you through positive, uplifting, and worshipful music. If you are listening to music that reinforces anger, revenge, bitterness, or depressing ideas, then remove that music from your life. It doesn't matter if you like it or it is your favorite band. If it encourages anger, then cancel that noise. There is so much good music out there of all different kinds of styles. Find some songs that lift you into the presence of God. I have found that good worship music can exorcise the thoughts and even the spirit of anger in my head.

FORMING NEW, POSITIVE THOUGHTS

Dear Lord Jesus,

I need new thoughts so I don't dwell on what makes me angry. I need new mental challenges that are positive. I need new dreams, ideas, and plans to be fully engaged with so that I don't focus on what happened in the past to "mess" up my present and future. You are the God of all wisdom and all power. Give me Your wisdom so my mind is not consumed in anger, bitterness, and vengeance. You are the God of all time. Give me a picture of a new future where my past grievances are forgotten, and the future is bright and loving.

In the Name of the Lord Jesus Christ, Amen

When God answers the prayer above and shows you positive things to do or think, write them down or note them on your phone. When God answers this prayer and gives you verses to memorize, start repeating them over and over again until they are memorized. It's okay if it takes a hundred times to say it over three months to get it memorized. Just get it in your brain to start battling for a clear mind. When God answers this prayer and has you hear a great worship song, add it to your streaming or purchase list to make a wonderful worship playlist when you need it.

D A Y

"DO NOT COMMIT MURDER" BEGINS WAY EARLIER THAN YOU THINK

Matthew 5:21-24

When I started playing tennis, I wasn't very good at it. A coach I had made our team significantly better by splitting the court in half and making us hit shots into only one half of the court. It shrunk the court and tightened my aim. We played many games on this narrow court, and when Coach finally let me play on the whole court, it seemed massive. This same technique is what Jesus is doing to help you with your anger. Many of us feel like we are okay with being angry as long as we don't kill anybody. But Jesus wants you to focus on controlling your anger so that you never have to worry about murder. He shrinks the court by telling us the penalties for any expressed anger.

In the Sermon on the Mount, Jesus had a serious discussion about anger under the topic of "murder." He knew the people of His day thought they were doing okay as long as they did not physically murder anyone during their lifetime. But God's standard is higher, so Jesus used this sermon to help them see that their way of thinking was unhealthy. God did not embrace the "Love Your Friends" and "Hate Your Enemies" slogans they thought were good morality. Look at what He actually said to the people about this issue of anger:

You have heard that the ancients were told, "You shall not commit murder" and "Whoever commits murder shall be liable to the court." But I say to you that everyone who is angry with his brother shall be guilty before the court; and whoever says to his brother, "You good-for-nothing," shall be guilty before the supreme court; and whoever says, "You fool," shall be guilty enough to go into the fiery hell. Therefore if you are presenting your offering at the altar, and there remember that your brother has something against you, leave your offering there before the altar and go; first be reconciled to your brother, and then come and present your offering.

(Matthew 5:21–24 NASB)

Jesus said that murder starts a lot earlier than you think it does. It begins with the anger and the hatred. He knows we need to cut off the anger at the roots so it never builds to the place of murder. God is not impressed by people who are barely holding back from physical murder while they rage at their enemies.

If we moved the ethical line from murder to revealed anger, we would have a different world. What if people were fined or taken to court for revealed anger? What if people were actually forced to apologize to people they had slandered? There have been times in various civilizations when what people said and did in anger was disciplined or not allowed. One of the miracles of civilized gatherings is that people can disagree but not resort to anger or violence.

Many times, we do not murder an actual person, but we do murder a relationship. It is commonplace in Western society to discard relationships because of our anger, contempt, defensiveness, lack of control, or cynicism. If we could treat expressed anger with the level of seriousness that Jesus ascribes to it, then we would be much more careful about what we say and do when we are irritated.

The interesting thing about the Matthew 5 passage is that many commentators tell us that this will be the ethical standard in heaven, but thankfully, we will not be as prone to anger as we are here. We will have emotions that will give us energy for change, but we will not demean others or think people are stupid just because they are different from us. Instead, we will protect the dignity of others and enjoy an abuse-free zone in heaven. People will respect differences and have different foci, even with the ultimate purpose of glorifying Jesus and doing His will. What a world that will be! It is what we strive for here in this world, but our sinful self-focus keeps getting in the way. Our souls and spirits are not strong enough to overcome our natural orientation to our flesh. That's why we need Jesus's help.

MEMORIZE GOD'S STANDARD FOR ANGER

1. Memorize Jesus's ethical lines and move your boundaries to His. Read this verse over and over out loud until you can say it without looking.

> But I say to you that everyone who is angry with his brother shall be guilty before the court; and whoever says to his brother, "You good-for-nothing," shall be guilty before the supreme court; and whoever says, "You fool," shall be guilty enough to go into the fiery hell.
>
> **(Matthew 5:22)**

Let these words rattle in your head for a few hours or a day. If you were to live by this level of accountability, how would you answer these questions?

- How many times would you have been hauled into court and convicted of being angry in public? Give an estimate of what that number would actually be. Don't just say "hundreds." Think through each time you let your anger out verbally or dismissively at someone else.
- Who comes to mind when you think of your most recent anger outburst?
- What do you need to no longer say about others?
- What could you say instead?

2. Confess each time that you have expressed anger verbally during the day.

Dear Lord Jesus,

I admit I called someone a fool, an idiot, or stupid today because they got in my way or did something I wouldn't do. I realize that it is wrong. Please apply the blood of

Christ to this sin in my life. I want to change the way I react. Please give me a new phrase to say. Show me what to do instead. Please keep working on me. Make me the kind of person you want me to be.

In the Name of the Lord Jesus Christ, Amen

CHANGING YOUR ANGER STANDARD TO GOD'S STANDARD

In this exercise, the goal is to change your standard of what an acceptable amount of anger is to Jesus's standard. We don't have this type of court and penal system at present, so you will have to set up some cost, punishment, or discipline to self-administer. What cost or discipline could you agree to if you violated Jesus's standard? Remember, this is a self-imposed system that causes you to think twice before you call someone an idiot, a fool, or stupid in public again. Here are some of the "fines" I gave myself while training away from anger.

- $100 for every infraction.
- Did the dishes after a meal for each infraction.
- Went without dessert for each infraction.
- Wrote out Matthew 5:21-24 five times for each infraction.
- Pulled weeds for ten minutes for each infraction.
- I rewarded myself $20 each time I withheld saying something when I wanted to let my usual moniker fly.

The point of this exercise is to move the win/lose anger line from where you have the line to where Jesus has it. What would make you remember to say something different? Was that the right thing or the wrong thing to do? What could you have done other than what you did? What needs to be done to you to cause you to make a different choice next time? What will you choose to say or do next time?

141

SEEING THE GOOD IN EVERYONE

Dear Heavenly Father,

I admit I am too quick to call someone an idiot or stupid. My attitude is murdering people through anger. I need You to help me see the good in everyone. I am too selfish. I need You to help me grow my patience with others who are in my way. Please come into my life at a new level and save me from my own destructive reactions. Thank You for dying on the cross for my sins. Show me how to start valuing others the way You do.

In Jesus's Name, Amen

D A Y
20

BECOME A PROBLEM SOLVER

James 1:2-3

The wonderful movie *Apollo 13* tells the true story of three astronauts who were stranded thousands of miles away from Earth in a crippled spaceship. They were supposed to go to the moon, but their oxygen tanks exploded, and they were facing certain death. They encountered problem after problem, none of which had been planned for by NASA. With each problem that arose, the head of all the departments would say, "Folks, work the problem!" "Don't get caught up in what can't be done." "Work the problem." At one point, the astronauts were being suffocated by CO_2. The engineers were assembled and told they had to clean the air on the spaceship with only the stuff in a box (stuff on the spaceship). They came up with a bizarre solution just in time before the astronauts suffocated.[16]

In the movie, the commander, James Lovell, stops the other astronauts from fighting about who caused the problem because he says they would still be here with the same problems after the fight, which wouldn't matter. He is right! It doesn't make sense to get angry as part of the solution to the problem. Anger and intense emotions usually just compound the problem and make you less able to think clearly.

You will face irritations, frustrations, and even significant issues that can trigger anger daily. Welcome them as friends to help you grow and strengthen your abilities and faith. We are like the driver on the freeway who thinks that if they can get around all of these cars, they will be in front, and it will be peaceful. There is no front of the freeway. There are always more cars. There are always more problems. Swatting a few problems away will not make our lives peaceful. There will always be more difficulties coming. We must learn how to be problem solvers for the endless stream of problems and issues that come at us, and doing so means we must get beyond our own opinions and ideas.

When all kinds of trials and temptations crowd into your lives my brothers, don't resent them as intruders, but welcome them as friends! Realise that they come to test your faith and to produce in you the quality of endurance. But let the process go on until that endurance is fully developed, and you will find you have become men of mature character with the right sort of independence.

(James 1:2–3 PHILLIPS)

When these difficulties come, we are often tempted to get mad and, in anger, force a quick fix on the problem. But I've found that anger often causes more problems than we realize. When we are angry, we are not solving the problem. We need to slow down and become problem solvers who do not react in anger.

The tendency with problems is to think that our initial idea or desire is the way to solve the problem. This may be true, but it rarely is the wisest way. If you are going to solve the problems in your life, you will have to look beyond your initial opinions and solutions. Your way feels right, but there are usually more options and better ways. Do not power up to get your way. Ask God to help you look at all the options. Be a part of the solution by considering the various ways to solve this issue.

I know how easy it is to get mad if we think our solution is so obvious that everyone should see it. We use anger to force our solution on others with little to no dialogue. Instead, we should use the opportunity to listen to others, be slow to anger, and gain wisdom. We should become someone who will help solve the problem, not just stir the pot with anger.

Proverbs 19:11 prompts us to use discretion about how we will handle our problems of the day. Ask, "What is my plan to deal with the problems coming today that I don't even know about yet?" Look at that simple five-step system again and do what it says. This problem-solving plan works every time. It is much better than an impulsive reaction or doing what you always do that never works.

When you successfully navigate a problem, it is helpful to review your progress toward your anger reset.

- What happened when you tried the problem-solving approach instead of the anger approach?
- What surprised you about the ideas of others when you started to ask for them?
- How difficult was it to let go of your solution and embrace a better one coming from someone else?
- Was it easier to stay calm because you were solving a problem rather than forcing your way?

Like the NASA engineers from Apollo 13, you can become a person who will "work the problem." Picture yourself as a man or woman of discretion, working through the various steps and understandings to handle the latest problem crowding your life. See yourself working through the steps. Resist engaging your anger to move things along. Stay calm, get the best minds in the game with you, come up with possible options, and move forward. This is how you refine your anger into mental and spiritual energy as you work through this proven problem-solving system.

THINK OPTIONS, NOT YOUR WAY

During my journey to overcome anger, I developed a simple way to solve problems that arise in my life. We all need some type of system to get beyond our own thinking. I hope you find this one useful.

Begin by writing these five steps and Proverbs 19:11 on a 3" x 5" card you carry with you or put in your phone so you can easily refer to them. These simple steps will force you to think beyond your own opinions.

1. Clarify the problem; don't guess or assume what it is.

2. Brainstorm possible solutions with wise people:

    a. Write down your initial thoughts about how to solve this problem.

    b. Ask people familiar with the problem about their understanding and possible solutions.

    c. Ask other wise people for their knowledge and ways to find a solution.

3. Narrow down the list of possible solutions in priority order.

4. Do the most potent option.

5. Be open to feedback on this solution as it is implemented.

"A man's discretion makes him slow to anger,
And it is his glory to overlook a transgression."
(Proverbs 19:11)

BECOMING A PROBLEM SOLVER

Dear Heavenly Father,

My selfish and foolish ways are producing anger in my life. Help me see the wise options that will keep me from anger long before I am angry. Let me be a more optional thinker rather than someone foolish if I don't get my way. Please come into my life at a new level and save me from my selfish point of view. Help me think of wise people I can go to when I need advice and solutions. Thank You for dying on the cross for my sins. Show me how to see more options.

In Jesus's Name, Amen

"MENTAL REHEARSAL IS THE BASIS OF THE PHRASE, 'WHAT WOULD JESUS DO?'"

—Gil Stieglitz

D A Y

21

MENTALLY REHEARSE MEEKNESS

Colossians 3:12–13

Jack Nicklaus, arguably the best golfer of all time, said that he never hit a ball in practice or a tournament without a picture of what he wanted it to do in his mind first.[17] He always had the mental picture first, then hit the shot. The mental image of the ball doing what he wanted it to do was crucial to his success.

Every Olympic athlete knows that to achieve their best performance, they must spend time picturing themselves doing a flawless performance. This is called mental rehearsal, our next strategy for resetting anger. Watching yourself do something flawlessly is not a waste of time; it's a crucial aspect of a better you. Nobody at the highest levels of performance would avoid rehearsals. Everyone who wants to be great rehearses in two ways: actual rehearsal and mental rehearsal. I am amazed that everyone knows this, but we do not think of doing this for our crucial relationships. We rehearse for presentations, pitches, and proposals but not for difficult moments in life where the life and death of a relationship is at stake.

Mental rehearsal is a form of biblical meditation, a topic we focused on in days 8 and 18. Colossians 3 instructs Christians to be kind, compassionate, patient, and loving, but this doesn't come naturally. We have to meditate on this verse and mentally rehearse what that looks like. This is the training we need to do to hear God's voice and feel His power in these crucial personal development arenas.

So, as those who have been chosen of God, holy and beloved, put on a heart of compassion, kindness, humility, gentleness and patience; bearing with one another, and forgiving each other, whoever has a complaint against anyone; just as the Lord forgave you, so also should you.

(Colossians 3:12–13)

If you remember the strategy of biblical meditation, we need to consider ourselves dead to the promptings of anger, lust, pride, and strife. God says we need to see ourselves responding to the promptings from the Holy Spirit to be meek, peaceful, joyful, and self-controlled instead. What would that look like if you were calm, peaceful, and self-controlled? If you cannot visualize yourself being calm, peaceful, and self-controlled, you will not be. Play the movie of you being calm, talking calmly, thinking through your actions, and remaining calm. It will never happen in real life until you can see it happening in your head.

Jesus says the same thing in Scripture:

Come to Me, all who are weary and heavy-laden, and I will give you rest. Take My yoke upon you and learn from Me, for I am meek and humble in heart, and you will find rest for your souls. For My yoke is easy and My burden is light.

(Matthew 11:28–29)

Mental rehearsal is the basis of the phrase "What would Jesus do?" and why everyone wore those bracelets many years ago. We must be able to see what Jesus wants us to do—to see ourselves actually doing what should be done. We need to see a mental picture of God the Holy Spirit empowering us to act in ways we have never acted before. Only then will we act the way God wants us to.

When you are tempted to express your anger, you need to have a mental picture of yourself reacting calmly and peacefully at the ready. Waiting until you are feeling angry makes it nearly impossible to create this picture. In the weeks and days before a tense situation, picture yourself choosing to die to that anger impulse and embrace relaxing your shoulders and speaking calmly.

See yourself being calm, relaxed, peaceful, and self-controlled through a tense meeting that is coming up. Picture what they will say. Picture your calm reaction. Picture their reaction to your new calm reaction. Picture what you will say. Picture what they will say because you are calm. Picture yourself taking the time to search for wisdom. Picture yourself ending the conversation or interaction in a very calm and self-controlled way. You must see yourself being calm. Play this movie in your head at least five times.

When you want to be defensive and point out what the other person did wrong, picture yourself listening to what they say and asking for more clarification. Picture yourself not reacting to what they say but trying to record or know their perspective. When someone is mad at you, this moment is not about you but about them. Picture yourself acknowledging their concerns and feelings. Picture yourself not being in a hurry to bring up your rebuttals, your point of view, your facts. Picture yourself putting that off until the next conversation. Picture yourself thinking, "They need to feel heard before I can share my perspective."

We are really talking about the spiritual attribute of "meekness." This is the ability to remain calm amid difficulty, anger, or frustration. What is the length of time that you can stay calm when it seems like the whole world is against you? Most see the wrong thing when something doesn't go our way. We see ourselves getting upset, yelling, walking away, or hitting something. This happens because this is what we see ourselves doing. But what if you could see yourself reacting differently to stressful situations? What kind of reaction would astound your spouse and colleagues and please God deeply? Begin rehearsing that kind of mental image.

To practice this discipline, consider whether you have role models who exercise meekness under pressure. If you haven't seen people handle difficult situations well, it will be harder to create a calm picture. You have to see what it looks like before you can do it. Who do you know who is calm under pressure? Ask if you can watch someone deal with a tense board meeting or difficult one-on-one. Don't say anything; just watch people do well in stressful situations. See the pressure they are under, and they are not giving in to it. Visualize yourself being meek when the pressure is on.

A famous example of a meek person is Tony Dungy, the Super Bowl-winning football coach. He was a man under control who never needed to raise his voice to get the players to perform at their best and win. He got his players to mentally rehearse every kind of play and situation they would face in the game to get ready. Consider studying more men like him, read their biographies, and learn about what makes them tick. Guys like Tony are great role models for those of us who are trying to manage our anger.

The Bible is also full of examples of people being meek. Think of Stephen as he was being stoned. The apostle Paul in the Philippian jail, and of course, Jesus, who exemplifies meekness:

"and while being reviled, He [Jesus] did not revile in return; while suffering, He uttered no threats, but kept entrusting Himself to Him who judges righteously;"
(1 Peter 2:23)

Below, I've listed some of the qualities of a meek person:

1. They are very intelligent.

2. They think before they act.

3. They are aware of many options.

4. They can be reasonable and bring results, unlike those who say a lot of nothing.

5. They are wise, using prudence, knowledge, and understanding to remain calm.

6. They let go of small fights.

EMBED MEEKNESS IN YOUR MIND

Repeat these Scripture verses and meditate on them until they become a part of you. Write them on a card you keep with you or on your phone.

Take my yoke upon you and learn of Me for I am meek and humble in heart.
(Matthew 11:29)

Blessed are the meek for they will inherit the earth.
(Matthew 5:6)

So, as those who have been chosen of God, holy and beloved, put on a heart of compassion, kindness, humility, gentleness and patience; bearing with one another, and forgiving each other, whoever has a complaint against anyone; just as the Lord forgave you, so also should you.
(Colossians 3:12–13)

VISUALIZE YOURSELF BEING MEEK

When you mentally rehearse being meek, visualize a movie in your mind. What does it look like to be powerful but under control? What does calm look like?

- At home, when everything is chaos ...
- At work, when people are upset ...
- Driving when lots of cars are on the roads ...
- Talking with a friend ...
- Working through a crisis ...
- Deciding what to do with new money ...
- Talking with God ...
- Being at peace with yourself ...
- When you are really hurried and stressed ...
- What do your shoulders do?
- What do your hands do?
- What do you say?
- What are you thinking?
- Are you sitting or standing?

HELP TO BE CALM UNDER PRESSURE

Dear Heavenly Father,

I want to have all my power under control. I want to be calm under pressure. I want my ability to change people and for things to be positive and not destructive. I need You, Lord Jesus, to be in me, with me, over me, and through me. Please come into my life at a new level and save me from my own destructive reactions. Thank You for dying on the cross for my sins. Make me the kind of person you want me to be.

In Jesus's Name, Amen

"DOES YOUR MOOD CHANGE WHEN YOU REMOVE YOURSELF FROM CERTAIN FRIENDS, FAMILY MEMBERS, OR COWORKERS FOR A PERIOD OF TIME?"

—Gil Stieglitz

D A Y

BE AWARE OF MIRRORING ANGER

Proverbs 27:19

A number of years ago, I was helping Jack and Debbie, who were having problems with their thirteen-year-old daughter, Samantha. She had always been helpful and respectful, yet now she was angry, hostile, and sarcastic toward her parents. It was like they had a different girl living in their house. She would slam doors and defiantly resist their direction. We looked at lots of other possibilities that could be causing this behavior change. Did something happen to her? Could this be because of something at home? Did something happen at school? Was this masking a need for independence? Could this be coming from the friends at school?

Everything changed when we tried a "friendectomy." Because of the increasing hostility in Samantha, we worked with the school to have her go on independent study for two weeks. She would not go to school or hang around with her friends from school. Remarkably, in a few short days, the delightful Sam re-emerged. She had been surrounded by angry, rebellious, and sarcastic friends, and she became like them. The parents changed the environment around their daughter, and the daughter returned to a normal young teenager. It was like a miracle.

In the 1870s, scientists discovered specialized neurons in the brain that control the ability to mimic, show empathy, and awareness of others' movements and moods.[18] These later became known as mirror neurons. We can take on the movements, emotions, and attitudes of others through the firing of these mirror neurons. This is what allows us to be social creatures. But it also can trick us into being angry because another person is angry or sad if the people around us are sad. Our mirror neurons help us learn new tasks and can help us understand the nonverbal signals that people are sending. We must use these strengths of mirror neurons without robotically mimicking the other person's emotions and actions. We are separate individuals in our adult friendships and groupings.

If you grew up in an angry family, then you may have adjusted to being angry. You will begin picking up their patterns and habits if you are around constantly irritable people. Whenever I mention that people should look at their friends, co-workers, and spouse as a source of their anger issues, it doesn't seem possible. But ask yourself: Does your mood change when you go away from friends, family, co-workers, or your spouse for a period of time?

I have watched teens become calm and pleasant when they get away from their parents. I have watched men and women become relaxed and calm when they spend a little time away from a micromanaging spouse. I have seen employees become different when put in different work groups or under different bosses. Can you change the environment you are living in?

I remember one business owner who wanted to fire an underperforming staff member. I suggested that the boss let the staff member know they should start looking for a new position outside the company to give the staff member some time to adjust to the new situation. Then, I was able to help the staff member find another job that came with a promotion and a raise. The business owner was very upset that this staff member, whom he wanted to fire, was getting a promotion and a raise. It had never occurred to him that the bad environment and underperforming staff resulted from his leadership style and the negative emotions in the office.

The book of Proverbs has several verses that bring out this issue of mirroring anger. You are not really angry, but anger is coming at you, and you are reflecting it back. Wouldn't you agree that it is sometimes hard to remain calm when the people around you are angry, nitpicking, frustrated, and attacking? Proverbs has many additional insights into this rarely discussed idea of mirrored anger.

> "As water reflects the face, so one's life reflects the heart."
> **(Proverbs 27:19 NIV)**

This verse provides individual insight into how whatever we let our soul focus on will be reflected in our mood or attitude. It also provides a larger insight into how the people around us can set our mood or attitude. In a sense, you are just reflecting back to people what you are getting from them.

Many times, your irritation is a reflection of the specific or general anger of the people around you. It is very easy to be like a mirror and reflect back the mood you are getting from others. This is a natural instinct. But you can choose not to be a reflector but a calm and peaceful force in other people's lives.

> "An angry man stirs up strife,
> And a hot-tempered man abounds in transgression."
> **(Proverbs 29:22 NASB)**

Notice this verse says that if you are around an angry person, there will be more strife and irritation than if everyone is calm. The anger of one person can trigger and grow the anger in others.

Many times, you are not angry, but because other people are picky, selfish, and irritable, you start becoming the same way. If someone points out something you did wrong, you immediately think of things they have done wrong or how they are irritating. We just reflexively do this to compensate. This starts a cycle of anger and irritability.

Realize that no one is really angry here; the atmosphere is charged with reactivity, and you can get swept up in it. Ask yourself, "Who is setting the mood in my life? Me or the people around me?" Choose the mood you want and fill your mind with the ideas, plans, and Scripture verses to bring that mood out.

"Do not associate with a man given to anger;
Or go with a hot-tempered man,
Or you will learn his ways
And find a snare for yourself."
(Proverbs 22:24-25)

God warns us that we will become like the people we surround ourselves with. Their actions, mannerisms, aggressiveness, and even anger will become woven into our actions and reactions.

This idea has enormous implications for our family-of-origin issues. Our parents or guardians programmed us in how to act, speak, and live life. If they were quick to anger, violent, or irritable, we adopted those patterns. We will need to unlearn these seemingly natural ways of living and diligently practice new responses and ways of thinking so we won't adopt the destructive patterns we learned in our family.

Have you ever had the experience of walking into a room and your mood changed almost immediately? You went from upset to calm, exhausted to relaxed, or too tired to energized? Realize that we are doing that to others, and they are doing that to us. So often, we do not pay attention to what the environment and people around us are doing to us. Your friends, co-workers, and family can be amping you up or feeding you their irritability. Most people find that if they hang around calmer people, they are calmer. If they hang around more disciplined people, they become disciplined. If they spend time with more successful people, they become more successful.

Anger is a reactive emotion. It is you reacting to the environment around you. If the environment is calm and peaceful, you are calmer and more peaceful. If the people and situation around you are irritable, frustrated, and angry, you can catch that infection from them.

EVALUATE THE EMOTIONS OF THE PEOPLE AROUND YOU

What infections are you catching from the people around you: joy or cynicism; love of learning or laziness; calm or irritability; future orientation or past obsession; peace or bitterness? Just like we can get diseases from other people, we can also catch their attitudes and dysfunctions. Take a hard look at the people you are around. Are they angry, dysfunctional, cynical, or positive, peaceful, and powerful?

Friends: Make a list of your friends and ask whether they are pushing you forward or holding you back.

1.

2.

3.

4.

5.

Family: Look at your reaction to your family members and their attitudes toward you.

1.

2.

3.

4.

5.

Coworkers: Are they increasing your joy, peace, and calm, or anger, irritability, and bitterness?

1.

2.

3.

4.

5.

Future friends and mentors: Who could you spend time with that would be a positive influence and provide an attitude adjustment?

1.

2.

3.

4.

5.

HELP ME NOT TO MIRROR OTHERS' EMOTIONS

Dear Heavenly Father,

I let other people's frustration and anger suck me into anger and frustration. Please give me wisdom and calm so that I do not mirror what other people are giving me. Show me how I need to prepare for various situations and people in my life. Show me when I need to make new friends and let others fall away. I want to actively choose my attitude and not let others infect me with their mood. Give me Your peace and calm even when things don't go smoothly. I ask that You show me when I am caught up in others' emotions. Show me how to die to their stimulation to anger and live in Your direction. Please forgive me when I have not been wise in this area.

In Jesus's Name, Amen

D A Y

PRACTICE GRATITUDE

Psalm 103:1-3

Bill was a driven and angry person. He was always striving for his business to get better and achieve all the goals he set for it, but it was never perfect, so he was always angry. Bill was part of a coaching group for business people. Because of his anger and negativity, the coach suggested that he change how he measured his life's accomplishments. Instead of measuring how far to go to a goal, he was to measure how far he had come from where he started. This idea revolutionized Bill's whole coaching group, except for Bill. He refused to acknowledge any progress until the goals were fully completed. He did not want to be grateful for making some progress or getting three-quarters of the way there—it was all or nothing. His coach warned him and the whole group that this attitude would destroy his business and probably his marriage and family if this attitude did not change. The coach was right: since Bill refused to change, he lost his business, his marriage, and his family.

We all need gratitude, and we must learn how to develop it. Gratitude is the beginning of the spiritual life.[19] The more gratitude you have, the less anger you have. Our brains cannot respond to negative emotions (fear, anxiety, stress) and positive emotions (gratitude) at the same time. So, if you're practicing gratitude, you have a way to reduce anxiety and feelings of overwhelm.[20] It takes training to become positive and grateful, but it can be done. One of the secrets to a much better life is trading your expectations for appreciation.[21] If you have eyes that see all the negative, you will constantly live in anger, bitterness, and cynicism. Let's be real. There is a lot that is wrong with our world. The Bible says it is because of the selfish and sinful choices of people over the years. A lot of sludge and corruption in our world has resulted from people making selfish and sinful choices. The Bible also says there is a lot of good in the world. We need to acknowledge the evil and the selfish but also see the beauty in our world. We can move out of a stream of selfishness and evil if we are caught in one. We need only to find the good and go after it.

One of the most practical books for growing gratitude is *The Gap and the Gain* by Dan Sullivan and Ben Hardy. This excellent business book helps entrepreneurs measure their progress instead of always measuring against the goals they have yet to reach. Happy people measure their progress.[22] Like our friend Bill, miserable people only measure their distance from the ideal. The Bible constantly reminds us to measure backward.

> How far have you come from when you started this battle with anger?

> How far have you come in expressing love and appreciation to your family?

> How far have you come in seeing the good all around you?

> How far have you come in whatever you are trying to accomplish?

We become grateful when we measure how much progress we have made instead of how far we are from the ideal. Of course, we would love to be already there or perfect in doing whatever it is, but that will leave us miserable.

The psalmist who wrote Psalm 103 is screaming at his soul to stop noticing all the negative and instead start noticing the positives, the blessings, the benefits, the healings, the lovingkindness, and the energy that comes from God. We need to train our eyes and souls to look for and notice the good in our lives.

> Bless the LORD, O my soul,
> And all that is within me, bless His holy name.
> Bless the LORD, O my soul,
> And forget none of His benefits;
> Who pardons all your iniquities,
> Who heals all your diseases;
> Who redeems your life from the pit,
> Who crowns you with lovingkindness and compassion;
> Who satisfies your years with good things,
> So that your youth is renewed like the eagle.
> **(Psalm 103:1-5)**

The apostle Paul tells us to dig hard to stay positive, to give thanks, and not to quench the Spirit. We take God's bounty for granted and refuse to look at what is good. Many of us can become fixated on something we don't have, refusing to see anything as positive until we gain that missing thing.

> Rejoice always; pray without ceasing; in everything give thanks; for this is God's will for you in Christ Jesus. Do not quench the Spirit.
> **(1 Thessalonians 5:16-19)**

Right after the longest discussion of overcoming anger in the Bible, the apostle Paul includes a crucial verse on kindness, gratefulness, and forgiveness. Without gratitude, we will not successfully control our anger or stop it at its source.

Let no unwholesome word proceed from your mouth, but only such a word as is good for edification according to the need of the moment, so that it will give grace to those who hear. Do not grieve the Holy Spirit of God, by whom you were sealed for the day of redemption. Let all bitterness and wrath and anger and clamor and slander be put away from you, along with all malice. Be kind to one another, tender-hearted, forgiving each other, just as God in Christ also has forgiven you.

(Ephesians 4:29-32)

Anger flows from ungratefulness. It flows from the negative, not the positive. Your anger comes from thinking you lack or were cheated out of something. The more your orientation is all that you have and all that you have gained, the less your anger will be triggered. You need to be able to say what is good about any situation. You need to be able to see the positives in every situation. You need to measure backward instead of forward toward an unreachable ideal. There are a couple of ways that you can use this insight:

1. When you are angry, irritated, and upset, you can force yourself to look at what you are grateful for. This can sometimes stop the boiling anger in your thoughts.

2. You can develop the habit of looking for and acknowledging what you are grateful for throughout your day. Stop and say, "What do I have now that I am grateful for?"

This gratefulness orientation will change your perspective. What good things do you notice God is sending your way? God's grace is getting more than you deserve. God has given us every spiritual blessing in the heavenly places (Ephesians 1:20) and constantly gives us good things (James 1:17). We need to find a way to live in gratefulness rather than greed and cynicism. This must become a way of seeing the world and living, not just having nice thoughts occasionally. In what ways have you gotten more than you deserve from God?

People tend to notice the big good things or things they have wanted for a while. It means we can easily look past small good things because they are not the big things we were focused on. God has been taking me through an exercise where I notice everything in my life and notice it for its blessing to me. I am slowing down and not hurrying to get the big thing so I'm not missing all the little blessings and the good that has already arrived in my life.

God's mercy is getting less than you deserve. God has forgiven you through the work of Jesus Christ for all of your sins. His forgiveness includes past, present, and future sins. His forgiveness releases you from any wickedness you committed, any trespasses you did, and all of your sins of omission that you commit constantly. His mercy overwhelms us, yet many of us bathing in the mercy of God still hold things against others. Jesus tells us to let go of our offenses in light of the offenses He has forgiven us for (Matthew 19). In what ways have you gotten less than you deserve?

God's patience is being given more time to cooperate with Him and His plans. In what ways have you received more time to cooperate with God on His plan?

EXERCISING YOUR GRATITUDE MUSCLES

Let's do a simple workout, some spiritual pushups, if you will. Write down ten things that you are grateful for. You can also make it more difficult by saying, "What are ten things I am grateful for that I can see or are around me right now." This simple gratefulness exercise will tone your spiritual muscles and get you in shape for a different life.

What are ten good things in your life right now?

1.

2.

3.

4.

5.

6.

7.

8.

9.

10.

HELP TO SEE THE GOOD THINGS IN MY LIFE

Dear Heavenly Father,

I ask that You give me eyes to see all the good things in my life. I realize that I regularly want and even demand unrealistic expectations, which triggers my anger. I want to be aware of the things that are already in my life that I have taken for granted. I want to be filled with gratitude for where I am now and the progress I have made from yesterday, last week, last month, and last year. You, Lord Jesus, are constantly streaming good things into my life, and I need to acknowledge and grasp them. I so often regularly push past Your good things to press on to things that I can't handle yet. Please forgive me for my anger and give me Your perception of the good things so I am filled with gratitude. I ask that You tear down the negative and cynical filters that hide Your grace, mercy, and patience toward me.

In the Name of the Lord Jesus Christ, Amen

"GOD DID NOT DESIGN US TO HANDLE BITTERNESS AND VENGEANCE."

—Gil Stieglitz

D A Y

RELEASE THE NEED FOR REVENGE

Romans 12:17-21

Winning at spiritual warfare demands that we remove bitterness from our hearts. Many of us don't think of bitterness as anger, so we overlook our reoccurring bitterness and our private desire for revenge. But if we are going to win the spiritual battle for a great Christian life, we must learn how to forgive. Someone once said that bitterness is like drinking poison and waiting for the other person to die. Letting go of bitterness is essential, but it is not easy.

In the classic book and movie *The Count of Monte Cristo*, Edmund Dantes, a righteous but naïve captain of a trading ship, is betrayed by his best friend and a crewmate. He is imprisoned for a crime he didn't commit by a corrupt prosecutor, his best friend marries his fiancé, and the crewmate takes over the shipping business. He loses everything and is confined for thirteen years in solitary confinement in Chateau D'if. His belief in God is destroyed, and he begins to live for revenge against the people who betrayed him. A priest, who is also falsely imprisoned, befriends him and mentors him to get ready for a new life. The priest and Edmund start working together to dig a tunnel to escape. The priest tries to get Edmund to let go of his revenge, but it is the only thing keeping him alive, and he won't let it go. Through a miraculous series of events, the priest dies, and Edmund escapes from Chateau D'if. Before dying, the priest tells Edmund of a great treasure and to only use the treasure for good, not for revenge. Edmund declares, "I will surely use it for my revenge." Edmund finds the treasure and uses the money to set up those who betrayed him to be destroyed. His plans for revenge are going perfectly, and then he finds love again. He realizes he can't have revenge and love simultaneously—he must choose one or the other. He must let go of his need for revenge and embrace love and even God again, or his bitterness will destroy him.

As this story shows, bitterness is one of the consistent places where anger hides. We don't think we are angry, but our anger has metastasized into bitterness. We long in our hearts for revenge against the person who wronged or blocked us. We do not believe we will be happy until we see the person who hurt us pay. If any of this sounds familiar, don't worry—bitterness can be defeated.

There are at least seventeen different ways of letting go of bitterness through the art of forgiveness. Here, I will only talk about one powerful way: giving all vengeance to God. I often call this process "Hiring God as Your Hit Man," where we let Him deal with what, when, and how justice and/or mercy is meted out. In Romans 12:17-21 (NASB), the Scriptures tell us,

Never pay back evil for evil to anyone. Respect what is right in the sight of all men. If possible, so far as it depends on you, be at peace with all men. Never take your own revenge, beloved, but leave room for the wrath of God, for it is written, "VENGEANCE IS MINE, I WILL REPAY," says the Lord. "BUT IF YOUR ENEMY IS HUNGRY, FEED HIM, AND IF HE IS THIRSTY, GIVE HIM A DRINK; FOR IN SO DOING YOU WILL HEAP BURNING COALS ON HIS HEAD." Do not be overcome by evil, but overcome evil with good.

God clearly tells us we are not designed to handle bitterness and vengeance. He knows these are corrosive emotions that will damage and even destroy the life you want. Sadly, most people collect hurts, wounds, and offenses. Rather than dreaming big dreams and going after them, their lives are about reacting, revenging, competing, or capitulating. So often, we believe that because of what others have done to us, we are stuck with the damage, the boundaries, and the future they put on us. But this is not true. There is another way. God asks us to let Him handle all justice and vengeance issues so we can start living a positive life and enjoying all the unique gifts, abilities, and opportunities He has given us.

What would happen if you let go of all the bitterness and start fresh with new dreams, goals, and purposes?

What if you turned over all justice and payback to God and moved beyond what they did to you?

Your life mission does not have to include payback to those who wounded you or blocked you. Everything in your life does not have to revolve around proving those people wrong, getting back at them, making them pay, or winning against them. STOP! This thinking aims you toward the wrong goals. Build your life to honor God and fulfill your unique purpose. Revenge is not a unique purpose.

What if God were to tell you that He would not step up to take care of the issue until you let go of the desire to be the blood avenger for the crimes committed against you? I have found that many times, I have wanted to be the one who delivered the pain and vengeance to the other person, but when I handed it over to God and let Him know that I would leave it with Him, He engaged and became my defender, protector, and avenger.

RELEASE THE NEED FOR REVENGE

This day's workout involves aiming for a great life free from bitterness and revenge. Today is when you start going after a good and righteous life. Yes, what this person did to you may have damaged one or more of your nine relational gardens, but it can be rebuilt and even be more magnificent. Let God have this issue of revenge. Accept that it will take everything you have to embrace all God has to build a life full of love, joy, and peace. Let payback go. If someone needs to be punished, stopped, or imprisoned, then God or His representatives will do that, not you.

Take a look at each of the relational gardens. What would your life look like if it were ideal in five years? Take some time to write down up to five things under each garden. Allow yourself to dream big in each one. If you have more time, brainstorm ten more.

THE IDEAL LIFE IN MY NINE RELATIONAL GARDENS	
In my marriage ...	• • • • •
In my family ...	• • • • •
In my work ...	• • • • •

THE IDEAL LIFE IN MY NINE RELATIONAL GARDENS

In my personal development/ achievement ...	• • • • •
In my finances ...	• • • • •
In my relationship with God ...	• • • • •
In my friendships ...	• • • • •
In my involvement with a church ...	• • • • •
In my involvement in my community ...	• • • • •

FREE ME FROM BITTERNESS

Forgiveness is often like a blind surrender—letting God know we will not pursue that person and trusting Him to do what is necessary. This releases us from being active agents in any justice so we can move on with living and filling our lives with love.

You may have to pray this prayer regularly until you stop holding the other person accountable for their actions. Remember, even if you get the desired revenge, pursuing it eliminates your ability to love and enjoy life. Don't let that happen.

Dear Heavenly Father,

I hand You my desire for revenge and payback against _____. I want to see them pay for what they did to me. I want to be the one who pays them back or sees them get what they deserve, but the more I pursue this, the less I seek the positive values and goals of my life. I need to have You handle my vengeance. I give these people to You to decide what justice, mercy, grace, or punishment they deserve. I want to get on with my life. You decide, God, what happens to them. I want to start filling my life with love, joy, and peace. I choose to let You handle all their issues. Show me whether this means reporting them to the right authority or letting You deal with this directly. I need to get beyond them. I will let You decide the measure of justice meted out to them. I need to be free of bitterness.

God, I am hiring You as judge, jury, and executioner of what happens to them. Show me how to begin this new life without this need for revenge. Show me the new relationships I need to pursue. Show me the new opportunities I need to explore. Show me how to think positively about my life. Show me how to dream big, positive dreams of a life filled with love. Thank You that You are for me.

In the Name of the Lord Jesus Christ, Amen

DAY

BRING ORDER TO THE CHAOS

Ephesians 6:15

I was fascinated to learn that race-car drivers usually walk the course they are about to drive, so they know every turn, pothole, and gravel spot on the track. They also go along the side of the track, knowing that if they are not prepared, they will not win. They review everything about the car and the race plan for that specific race. Nothing can be left to chance if they want a chance of winning.

As Christians, we run a race daily, attempting to live out Christ's love, righteousness, and peace (Hebrews 12:1–3). But maybe the goal of our race (the "winning") is in the preparation more than the actual race, for it is the preparation that allows us to win over anger.

One thing I have noticed is that angry people are often disorganized and impulsive. We can decrease our anger by being more organized and prepared for what life throws at us. We can do this by practicing shalom—peace.

Many people know *shalom* is the Hebrew word for peace, but it also carries the idea of order, harmony, and the lack of chaos.[23] So many times, we become angry because of the chaos in our lives. We hope things will work out just right so we can do whatever we want, but a hundred things get in the way. Then we get flaming angry because something got in the way of our perfect plan. But our chaos sabotages the plan because we don't remove the disorder before we start. Maybe we don't give ourselves extra time, get the right tools for the job, or communicate very much with the other people who are crucial to the completion of the plan. We don't think through what could go wrong with the plan before we start or ask enough other people about our possible plan. We just impulsively launch into the plan without preparing.

This idea of preparation is found in one of the pieces of the armor of God given to us in Ephesians 6:15—"Having shod your feet with the preparation of the gospel of peace." If we are going to bring peace to a situation, we must prepare beforehand. The enemy attacks us and wants us to blow up and spew our anger everywhere. His goal is to see us fail. But God wants us to make progress by loving people and promoting righteousness. The devil knows he can derail all the good you intend by having the chaos and disorder in your life set you off. He wants you to keep being impulsive. He wants you to ignore preparation and planning. He wants you to continue to think a good idea is enough. So if we are going to be peaceful people, we must begin to clean up the chaos and disorder of our lives.

Shalom is the opposite of chaos. God wants us to move toward shalom and live in peace with Him and others, which means the opposite of disorder and chaos. Too often, we don't want peace, though; we want our way amid chaos. Our job is to push for peace by preparing well. We remove the obvious aspects of disorder from our lives so we can reset our anger. We have systems in place to prepare us for a successful, anger-free day, and we remove all the obstacles that have derailed us in the past. Some basic systems might be:

- Getting up on time to have an unhurried approach to each day.

- Picking up after yourself when you make a mess instead of telling yourself you will get to it later.

- Planning out how you will instruct your children about homework, expectations in a social setting, or a chore or repair around the house.

- Keeping a tidy room or workspace.

- Planning to leave for an appointment with more than enough time to get there, considering if there is traffic. (See Day 11.)

Change the level of preparation, and you will reset your anger. Communicate ahead of time with your spouse, children, colleagues, and bosses, and you will reset your anger. Take the time to have an ordered workspace, and you will reset your anger. Take the little time it takes to wash the dishes or clean the counters every day, and you will reset your anger. What are the obstacles that regularly get in your way? Traffic, children, can't find your papers, gravity, colleagues? Think through how you can bring order to the chaos of doing these things and interacting with these people. What would it take to eliminate obstacles before starting this new plan?

The people who are often the most calm have set aside time to get ready to work and clean up their work. These people spend half an hour to an hour getting ready and cleaning up. It is just built into their way of operating, and this extra time allows them to be calm.

I remember working with this exemplary road crew in Roseville, CA. The head of the crew was incredibly calm, thorough, and well-respected. He would talk with the neighbors before a project was launched and put up signs that said a road project was coming. He would set up the crew for the work, explaining what would be done that day. He would let them know when clean-up would start at the end of the day. On Friday, he also had the whole crew clean the machines for the next week. It was one of the best-running and cleanest road crews I have ever seen. They were never flustered, and the project ran smoothly. This kind of order is possible for you too.

BRINGING ORDER TO THE CHAOS

Today's workout involves thinking and writing. You can use your own piece of paper or the workspace below. Write across the top the areas that often make you angry. These could include traffic, the children, work, your spouse, a hobby, or talking with a particular person. Brainstorm the various areas where you notice disorder and chaos contributing to the problem. Each area where you regularly get angry is a separate heading.

Ask yourself, "How can I bring order to these areas or situations so that I won't get angry?" The answer will not be, "They should just do what I say." Think through what new things you could do or say or not do or say that would allow you to remain calm, even if they acted the same way they usually did. You are looking for new ways to prepare so things will go more smoothly, and so the impulse of anger won't rise up.

Areas Where I Regularly Get Angry				

How Can I Bring Order to These Areas or the Situation? What Preparations Can I Make?				

Now, implement your solutions to bring order to the situation and see if they help you remain calm. Keep looking for new ways of speaking, acting, and preparing to maintain a calm demeanor.

I remember when our children were growing up, I would get angry that they were acting up again. My wife and I figured out that we needed to have a family staff meeting to discuss what we would do if they misbehaved. She wrote what we agreed on and how to correct the behavior on a card and posted it on the refrigerator for everyone to see. This helped me tremendously to stay calm as we trained our children in an orderly way to be civilized and delightful. We brought order to the chaos by preparing the correction in advance instead of trying to think of something on the fly.

Remember, if you regularly find yourself angry, there is some level of chaos in your situation that needs to be removed to remain calm. If you really want to be peaceful, you will have to do some work to remove elements of chaos and disorder. A new and calmer you will have more routines and spend more time preparing and cleaning up.

Celebrate every day that you did not get externally angry. It is a big deal that you did not get angry on that day. Kudos to you! We may never be perfect, but every day without anger is a good day. When we prepare to win that day, it deserves a celebration. Each day is one lap of the race. Prepare to win today. You can remain calm because you have eliminated disorder and chaos. You have given yourself enough time. You have communicated. You have consulted with wise people about your idea. You educated your team members ahead of time. You won over anger today!

> Having shod your feet with the preparation of the gospel of peace.
> **(Ephesians 6:15)**

LET ME HAVE MORE SHALOM IN MY LIFE

Dear Heavenly Father,

I come in the Name of the Lord Jesus Christ, asking You to show me where I need to remove levels of chaos and disorder that encourage anger. I realize that I have allowed disorder and a lack of planning to make me rush into my plans. It is this rushing, disorder, and lack of communication that causes the chaos and pushes my anger to the surface. I need Your help and energy to clean up these areas of disorder and lack of planning. Help me slow down and think through what needs to happen before, during, and after so that I will remain calm. I need You to show me what needs to be changed and give me the energy to do that work. I want shalom in my life, and my current way of living will not produce the peace I want.

Amen

D A Y

OVERCOME THE GOLDEN CHILD SYNDROME

Proverbs 3:7

Whenever my wife and I take a road trip, I like to prepare some questions ahead of time to help make the trip go faster and full of quality time. On one trip, I asked my wife a question that led to an incredibly powerful three-hour discussion. I asked, "What are three childhood memories you have never told me about before?" She began by pulling out the normal memories I had heard many times before, but this question forced her to think of memories we had never discussed in our decades of marriage. She shared all kinds of memories of her elementary and pre-school years. It was delightful and enlightening. She then asked about my childhood memories that I had never shared with her. I talked about memories with a best friend, where every day we would get into a fistfight before lunch, separate for lunch, but then get together in the afternoon like nothing had happened.

It turned out that both of us got angry every day as children. Wondering why this was, we discovered that both of us had been the "Golden Child" or the favored child of the family. We were used to getting our way, and our parents tended to let us have our way. We realized that our well-meaning parents had almost guided both of us to expect that we would get what we wanted. But when we went out in the real world of other real people, our mental framework didn't work. We had a rough time making friends because nobody did what we wanted.

It took me much longer to overcome this "Golden Child Syndrome" than my wife. I still fight those old tapes in my head regularly— "They should just do it my way." In my work with all kinds of people on this issue of anger, I have noticed that some people who have the worst problem overcoming their anger are those who have this Golden Child Syndrome. They have been almost programmed by their parents, teachers, coaches, or youth leaders that they should get their way. When this kind of programming comes up against other people who also think they should get their way, the anger comes out quickly.

"Why aren't they fawning over my idea?"

"Why aren't they asking me what I think?"

"Why am I not on that team or leadership group?"

Proverbs 3:7 is a helpful reminder not to be wise in our own eyes. The Bible clearly states that all of us must humble ourselves under the mighty hand of God and His ways for life to work. We must overcome this idea that "people should just do things my way." If we look at the Scriptures, we see that Joseph was the Golden Child in Jacob's family. He could do no wrong. God was even giving Him dreams and visions of power. Joseph's pride and showy arrogance are what caused his brothers to sell him into slavery in Egypt. He only learned humility through the difficult times he experienced there.

Moses was another man who was a Golden Child. He was entirely favored by his parents and by Pharoah's family. When He came of age, he thought everyone should just do what he wanted, which caused him to slay the Egyptian and hide his body in the sand. He had to be humbled, and his forty years in the wilderness did that.

David also became a Golden Child after Samuel anointed him the next king of Israel. His brothers treated him rough, and King Saul elevated him but then humbled him by chasing him all over the land and seeking to kill him for years. The programming of the Golden

Child must be tempered by humility, or it is unusable.

The worst case of the Golden Child Syndrome told in Scripture is Lucifer, the anointed cherub. Ezekiel 28 goes out of its way to tell us how beautiful, wise, and powerful this angelic being was. It also tells us that he refused to submit to the ways and order of God. He rebelled and wanted to be God in his own right. God created him and gave him spectacular gifts, but he used those to convince himself that he did not need to do things God's way. His was the first sin. He incited violence against God because he wanted all of his ideas and thoughts to be accomplished.

The Golden Child Syndrome will direct you to anger because you are used to getting your own way. You must become humble enough to realize that you may be a leader, but not everything you think or say is good. Your opinion should not always win. Your leadership must marry wisdom and be open to other ideas and additions. You must be willing to be disagreed with without getting angry.

Winston Churchill's father, John Randolph Churchill, was expected to become Prime Minister of England during his lifetime. He was a towering intellect and a forceful person. He was elected to Parliament and headed to fulfill his destiny. He became head of finances for his party and the nation at an early age. At one point, he submitted a budget for the country that his prime minister rejected. He was so aghast that his budget and solutions were rejected that he resigned. He had expected this would be such a shock that they would beg him to reconsider and return. Instead, his resignation was accepted, and he was out of Parliament, never to return. He ran several times but was never elected again. He destroyed his destiny because of his anger over one of his ideas being rejected. He was a Golden Child who destroyed his potential through his anger.

I have watched several Golden Children destroy their own potential because they cannot control the ideas that have been instilled in them that everyone should do what they say. Golden Children can have a huge positive impact on the world, but they must be willing to submit to reality, humble, and wise. They must also overcome their tendency to anger when things don't go their way.

LEARNING TO MODERATE REALITY, HUMILITY, AND WISDOM

There are three things that a Golden Child must learn to moderate: reality, humility, and wisdom. When you have the messages in your head that you are a person of destiny, you must let reality, humility, and wisdom inform your ideas and plans.

What is reality telling me?

_____

_____

_____

Understanding what God is doing What does humility tell me right now?

_____

_____

_____

Understanding what God is doing What is wisdom saying?

_____

_____

_____

Understanding what God is doing If you are a Golden Child or a favored one, God has likely been trying to help you shape that natural drive for constructive purposes, not selfish ones. It's important to realize how God has been trying to train, humble, and inject wisdom into you. Remember that Hebrews 12:6 says God disciplines the child in whom He delights. Yes, there are promotions you will not get and relationships that won't go your way. There are menial jobs you need to go through, and there will be periods of loneliness and even exile. If you've experienced such trials, what was God trying to do in and through you during these times? Were you listening? How has God been trying to train you, humble you, and inject wisdom into you?

_____

_____

_____

Understanding what God is doing to help you fulfill your destiny and cooperate with Him rather than resist Him can be very important. Remember, He is interested in you embracing reality, humility, and wisdom. Right now, He is working with you through the opportunities, difficulties, and trials in your life (James 1:2,3).

HELP ME NOT TO BE WISE IN MY OWN EYES

Dear Heavenly Father,

I come in the Name of the Lord Jesus Christ and have become aware that I often act out of my innate sense that I am always right. I am not right all the time, as You well know. I make a mess of things when I push for my own way. I need You to help me harness these strong opinions and sense of destiny. I get angry too often when I don't get my way. I act like a spoiled brat. I need to learn to live in the real world, where there are many forces that will not bend to my will. I need to walk humbly with others, not always asserting my ideas and ways but showing interest in their ideas and stories. I need Your wisdom, Lord Jesus, to create a better future for everyone around me, including myself. I admit that I am often tempted to fight for my way instead of Your way of Wisdom. Show me how to walk with You in humility and wisdom. I freely admit that I need You directing my life and not just my own ideas.

Amen

D A Y

BATTLE AGAINST YOUR TEMPERAMENT REACTIONS

James 4

We have nearly reached the end of this book on resetting anger. We have examined various techniques and exercises for conducting spiritual warfare against your tendency toward anger. I hope you have found at least seven to ten spiritual exercises to help you downregulate your anger.

For this last chapter, I want to review James chapter 4, a hidden gem regarding conquering anger. One of the things that is true of many of us who struggle with anger regularly is that we have a temperament or personality that wants to be in charge or in control or empowered in some way. Anger is the default mechanism that leaks out when things don't go our way. We have to recognize that something in our personality almost demands that we get our way. Sometimes, this is good; many times, it is unnecessary or can be bad. This chapter in James exposes this temperament issue and gives us nineteen insights to deal with this internal drive to get our way even when it is not helpful.

Psychologists tell us there are three basic temperament motivations: agency, bonding, and certainty. Each can be expressed in three different ways or nine different temperament patterns. If you are motivated by seeking agency and you are blocked, your default reaction is anger. If your normal motivation is for bonding and you are blocked, the default reaction is sadness or sorrow. If your normal motivation is for certainty and you are blocked, then your default reaction is fear.[24]

I want to walk through the biblical admonitions from James 4 to those seeking agency, power, empowerment, or control. You, like me, will regularly feel anger when you don't get the agency you are looking for. You will need to use the techniques in this book and the specific insights here to downregulate your anger so your personality does not destroy your destiny. You were made to lead, yet your natural flaring of anger will destroy your relationships and opportunities. Read through this chapter and use these insights from God about your temperament problem. Also, many books deal with temperament issues that naturally move to anger. I invite you to check them out.

James 4

[1] What is the source of quarrels and conflicts among you? Is not the source your pleasures that wage war in your members? [2] You lust and do not have; so you commit murder. You are envious and cannot obtain; so you fight and quarrel. You do not have because you do not ask. [3] You ask and do not receive, because you ask with wrong motives, so that you may spend it on your pleasures. [4] You adulteresses, do you not know that friendship with the world is hostility toward God? Therefore, whoever wishes to be a friend of the world makes himself an enemy of God. [5] Or do you think that the Scripture speaks to no purpose: "He jealously desires the Spirit which He has made to dwell in us"? [6] But He gives a greater grace. Therefore, it says, "GOD IS OPPOSED TO THE PROUD,

BUT GIVES GRACE TO THE HUMBLE." [7] Submit therefore to God. Resist the devil and he will flee from you. [8] Draw near to God and He will draw near to you. Cleanse your hands, you sinners; and purify your hearts, you double-minded. [9] Be miserable and mourn and weep; let your laughter be turned into mourning and your joy to gloom. [10] Humble yourselves in the presence of the Lord, and He will exalt you.

[11] Do not speak against one another, brethren. He who speaks against a brother or judges his brother, speaks against the law and judges the law; but if you judge the law, you are not a doer of the law but a judge of it. [12] There is only one Lawgiver and Judge, the One who is able to save and to destroy; but who are you who judge your neighbor?

[13] Come now, you who say, "Today or tomorrow we will go to such and such a city, and spend a year there and engage in business and make a profit." [14] Yet you do not know what your life will be like tomorrow. You are just a vapor that appears for a little while and then vanishes away. [15] Instead, you ought to say, "If the Lord wills, we will live and also do this or that." [16] But as it is, you boast in your arrogance; all such boasting is evil. [17] Therefore, to one who knows the right thing to do and does not do it, to him it is sin.

Many truths in James 4 are spelled out clearly and powerfully for those of us who want agency, empowerment, and control and find it easy to express anger when we don't get these things. In this section, I will go verse by verse and expound on the nineteen insights James offers. It will help you **read the verse, think about the questions, and consider what steps or actions you can take to do it.** I know some of this will be repetitive to the other lessons in this book, but isn't it interesting how the word of God works like that? Enjoy!

DOING BATTLE WITH YOUR ANGRY TEMPERAMENT REACTIONS

1. Examine where your anger is coming from.

> "What is the source of quarrels and conflicts among you? Is not the source your pleasures that wage war in your members?"
>
> **(James 4:1)**

a. Is your anger coming from a selfish desire for control, or what is best for everyone?

b. If it is from selfishness, confess that to God and yourself.

Learn to let your anger go if it is for selfish purposes of control or power. Many anger addicts have learned how to grasp this impulse toward anger that rises within them and downregulate it as they realize getting angry will not move the relationship or the situation forward. You don't have to let anger flare when you don't get your way. We have allowed our anger to flare often because it is easy and almost always available to us, but we have also learned it is often not helpful.

Those of us who get angry easily and often are just angry because we didn't get our way. Someone or something is resisting what we want to happen. Stop and admit that your anger is selfish. Let it go. It is foolish to believe that you will always get what you want. No one does.

2. Stop using anger to intimidate others.

> "You lust and do not have; so you commit murder. You are envious and cannot obtain; so you fight and quarrel."
>
> **(James 4:2)**

a. How often do you resort to violence or threats to get your way?

b. Instead of resorting to anger, ask yourself, "How can everyone win in this situation?"

Using violence, the threat of violence, or the look of potential violence is not the way to peace or godliness. There is another way, a much better way … the way of WISDOM. We need to downregulate our anger to make a persuasive case, not upregulate it. Too many people have always upregulated their anger, and it has become a part of their temperament pattern.

Make no mistake—someone convinced against their will is still of the same opinion. If you use your anger, violence, or a weapon, like a gun, to force people to do what you want, they will resent you and not be able to have a trusting relationship with you. They are just waiting for you to fly off the handle again. They are also waiting to flee the relationship. I have talked with many men and women who were devastated when their spouse, children, or employees left because they had had enough of their partner's, parents', or boss's anger. Angry people are just so used to seeking agency in every situation that they think anger is the quickest and best way to get it. It isn't. It is toxic and abusive in most cases.

3. Anger is poor communication.

"You do not have because you do not ask."
(James 4:3)

a. Do you tend to vomit your anger on everyone?

b. What do you remember about the "Seek wisdom, not your own way" principle?

Practice talking through things and listening to the other person instead of venting your anger. Discuss your desires, interests, and ideas. Discuss their desires, interests, and ideas fully: "Here is what I am thinking." "What do you think about this?" "Of these three options, which one sounds best to you?"

If you think you're a good listener, you're probably not. Learn to listen more. Probe their answers to understand what they are thinking and why. Ask them to share more by asking more questions. Don't interrogate them to win an argument. Listen.

To share your perspective, ask them first if they are open to another perspective. Only if they say yes can you share your ideas and points of view. Make sure that they feel heard and that you have grasped what they are thinking and feeling. This will also allow you to slow down any angry response.

On the journey toward wisdom, asking for other people's thoughts and perspectives often creates peace and better outcomes. Share your ideas; don't just throw them at people. Your ideas may be the best, and others may have even better ideas. Some combinations of ideas may prove to be the most practical. Spend some time looking for new ideas and solutions.

4. Ask for positive and wise changes instead of negative or selfish things.

"You ask and do not receive, because you
ask with wrong motives, so that you may
spend it on your pleasures."

(James 4:3)

a. What are your motives behind your requests or demands?

b. How can you state what you want positively and calmly?

It is easy to think of what you want to stop or the negative things you want, but real change will only begin when you understand what positive and wise changes you need to pursue. Your requests of God and others are often selfish and negative, full of wrong motives and your own pleasures. It is no wonder they are resisted or rejected. It's time to let go of what is selfish and unrighteous. It is toxic and will not ultimately benefit you.

I've often found that people are not ready to ask for something to change until they can state what they want in a positive request. God wants us to ask for what we want, not what we don't want (Philippians 4:6-8). Learn to ask God and others for what you righteously and positively want.

Dear Heavenly Father,

I come in the Name of the Lord Jesus Christ asking You for these positive changes to my life: _____; _____; _____. I realize it is easy to be negative, and I want Your wisdom to know how to understand and ask for what I positively need rather than just wanting something negative to stop or someone else to change.

In Jesus's Name, Amen

5. Move toward God and righteous desires rather than your selfish desires.

> "You adulteresses, do you not know that
> friendship with the world is hostility toward God?
> Therefore, whoever wishes to be a friend of the world
> makes himself an enemy of God."
> **(James 4:4)**

a. Are you a friend or foe of God? How can you know?

b. How much do you rely on the world to meet your physical, emotional, mental, and spiritual needs?

Jewish literature discusses the duality of our souls and bodies by picturing a man riding a donkey. The man is your soul, and the donkey is your body. The donkey wants to do all kinds of things that are not the plans for the man, but the donkey must be under the man's control, not the other way around.[25]

We have all known people who were on fire for God at one point in their lives, but they allowed the temptations of parties, houses, affairs, alcohol, pleasure, etc., to take them away from interacting with God and doing His things. It is like people who are world beaters at the board game Monopoly but are not skilled in real life. They may be good at the stuff and glamor of this life but have nothing good toward God. Become God's friend by doing righteous and helpful things for others. If you let the world try and meet your needs, you will not be a friend of God. Stop letting the donkey decide your path ... use your reason, wisdom, and spirit.

6. God wants a relationship with you.

> "Or do you think that the Scripture speaks to no purpose: 'He jealously desires the Spirit which He has made to dwell in us'?"
>
> **(James 4:5)**

    a. How often do you engage with God by allowing Him to lead, guide, and empower you?

    b. Do you have an interactive relationship with Him? How can you know?

God will not be your genie who grants you wishes, wants, or pleasures. As He was with Abraham, He wants to be our friend and partner in building a life that would not otherwise be possible. We often think we can do some part or all of life on our own, with our desires and thoughts directing us, but we cannot.

One of the great things that has allowed me to downregulate my anger is engaging with God every day. One year, I read through the Proverbs. Every day, I would ask God to help me answer my number-one question that would likely be coming that day or the next. I would read through the Proverb for the day and prayerfully look for God's answer. He would always highlight verses that spoke to that issue in my life. If the answer was not in the Proverbs, it was usually in Psalms or some other book of the Bible that God directed me to.

The fact that I can meet with God daily, where I get information, direction, and even warnings about the stuff that I face, makes my relationship with God alive. That year, I was amazed at how often, especially at the beginning, the verses He pointed out had to do with controlling anger, being careful with what I said, not being selfish, or not being arrogant. Those instructions were what I needed, even though I didn't know it until God pointed it out in the Scriptures.

7. **God is against you when you are proud, self-centered, and ungrateful.**

> "But He gives a greater grace. Therefore, it says, 'GOD IS OPPOSED TO THE PROUD ...'"
>
> **(James 4:6)**

a. How often do you find yourself constantly demanding to get your way? Do you believe pride is a factor?

b. How open are you to other ideas and other perspectives?

When you allow pride to dictate getting your way, you can bet God will oppose you in these self-centered activities. Anger puffs up your ego, and you lose perspective, so God says He will resist you in accomplishing your goals. Turn off your anger and arrogance, and let God's grace and wisdom help you.

Look for the ways that God is opposing you because of your pride, sinful desires, and lack of teachability. Realize that until you seek out other perspectives and other people's good and your own, God will be opposed to you.

8. **Open yourself to God's favor by being teachable, grateful, and adaptive.**

> "... BUT GIVES GRACE TO THE HUMBLE."
>
> **(James 4:6)**

199

a. Who can you learn from in a situation that makes you angry?

b. How can you adapt to the reality of the situation instead of demanding your way?

For thousands of years, mankind has walked by vast treasures of energy and blessings hidden all around them. Then, some people began to harness wind power to sail the seas. Others began to harness the power of waterfalls to turn wheels. Still, others discovered the power packed in oil and tar to light the evening and create engines. In the same way, many people are walking past the energy and favor of God that resides in seeking multiple perspectives, being willing to learn new things, and adapting to the reality of the people and circumstances they are facing. God is waiting to give you this favor and energy to power your life so you can go places and achieve beyond what you can dream.

9. God is in control, and you are not.

"Submit therefore to God."

(James 4:7)

a. What would a submissive person do in the situation you are facing?

b. What does God want you to do before, during, and after this circumstance that usually causes you to blow up?

It's time to start acting like God is in charge, not you. Remind yourself that you submitted to God, and you must act differently than you did before when you thought you were in charge. Pray a prayer of submission to God each time you start doing things your own way.

Dear Heavenly Father,

I come in the Name of Your Son, the Lord Jesus, and submit to Your ways and Your wisdom in this situation that regularly makes me angry. I need to see other perspectives. I need to adapt to the real situation instead of just bellowing against the way things are now. I need to search for things I can be grateful for in this situation.

Amen

10. Resist the impulse to be angry, and do not let your anger out.

"Resist the devil, and he will flee from you."

(James 4:7)

a. How is the devil tempting you to show your anger and demand your way?

b. How will you refuse to let the devil use your body and mouth to spew your anger?

If you are a person who tends toward anger, there is likely a pressure building inside of you where your anger might come spilling out. It is what you have always done, but now you will not act that immaturely. You are battling the devil and listening to God. Hold back the devil's suggestions. Listen to God's direction and do those quickly. Just like you learn to resist the urge to go to the bathroom whenever you feel like it, you must resist the desire to be angry anytime you feel like it. Grow up!

11. Engage your relationship with God when tempted to anger.

"Come close to God and He will come close to you."

(James 4:8)

a. When you get angry, have you asked God what He wants you to do instead of getting angry?

b. Do you listen to the thoughts and images that come to your mind and do them?

When we approach God from a learning, submissive position, He will show up. Having a relationship with God is slightly different from most relationships because God can put thoughts in our minds. We will not see someone talking to us or hear an audible voice, but we can still interact with Him. He brings Scriptures to our mind. He puts images in our minds to direct us. He puts thoughts in our minds to act on. He reminds us of emotions and incidents to redirect our emotions. Instead of being too consumed by the emotions of anger, lust, gluttony, ego, or greed, engage your relationship with God and do what He is prompting you to do.

12. Confess your sins of anger.

> "Cleanse your hands, you sinners; and purify your hearts, you double-minded ..."
>
> **(James 4:8)**

a. How easy is it for you to agree with God that whatever angry thing you did was wrong, not just a mistake that can be brushed aside?

b. Do you practice confessing your wrongs to God?

Each time you express anger at others, the best thing to do is immediately tell God it was wrong. There must be another way to handle disappointment, unrealistic expectations, and difficulty, and He knows the answer. If you do not admit this was the wrong way to handle the issues, you'll just keep doing them. There must be a cost, and I think you'll agree that a prayer of confession is a very small cost.

Dear Heavenly Father,

I come in the Name of the Lord Jesus Christ to admit to You again that I let my anger out through my speech or actions. It was wrong when I said _____ or did _____. Show me what I could have done differently. Show me how to take a different path next time.

Amen

13. **There must be real contrition and sadness over what you have done to others.**

> "Be miserable and mourn and weep;
> let your laughter be turned into mourning
> and your joy to gloom."
> **(James 4:9)**

a. How aware are you of how your anger affects the people in your life?

b. Do you notice the look on their faces or the words they say back? Can you visualize your last angry altercation?

We must realize how this sin threatens our awareness of God and our relationships with others. Our anger is like a flame thrower spewing flames at others; we must realize its damage.

This verse invites you to feel the stupidity of this childish way of acting. Take the time to feel the emotions of those who experienced your withering anger. Walk in their shoes and imagine them waiting for you to blow up. Remember when others have blown up at you and how you felt.

14. **Wait for God to exalt you instead of pushing for your own glory.**

> "Humble yourselves in the presence
> of the Lord, and He will exalt you."
> **(James 4:10)**

a. Can you serve others with humility and practice patience, waiting for the Lord to act versus taking matters into your own hands?

b. Do you seek the validation of others for your worth or approval?

Grasping and scheming to be respected, honored, or exalted is not God's way and will not result in what you want. It often creates a game of constantly needing others to validate your worth instead of serving, loving, and knowing it.

Waiting for God to lift you up usually requires a significant amount of time worshiping God or delighting in Him. He has said in Psalm 37:4 that if we delight in Him, He will give us the desires of our hearts.

It is often tough for the activistic person to wait. We want to make whatever is to happen now. Learn how to pray, prepare, and act when the time is right. Being godly means being willing to serve God and others and patiently wait for the right time. Some people wait too long, but those with a consistent problem with anger are not those people. We typically act too fast without the right amount of preparation. Take the lower place and serve others. Develop friendships and display virtue and character, realizing that God sees everything. He will prompt you when it is time to act. The place of humility is a great place to rise up from when it is time to move forward.

15. Stop using slander, gossip, and negative observations to let your anger out.

> "Do not speak against one another, brothers
> and sisters. The one who speaks against a brother
> or sister, or judges his brother or sister, speaks against
> the law and judges the law; but if you judge the law,
> you are not a doer of the law but a judge of it.
> There is only one Lawgiver and Judge, the One
> who is able to save and to destroy; but who are
> you, judging your neighbor?"
> **(James 4:11-12)**

a. Do you tend to fixate on the negative aspects of other people?

b. How much do you think anger has to do with this?

Many people don't think they are angry when saying negative things about others. But it is anger that motivates this negative and slanderous impression. Unless the person is doing wicked things or about to harm another, there is no need to give a bad report about someone. And even then, only report the potential evil to the proper authorities who can stop the wickedness.

Stop looking at the negatives in other people's lives. Look for the positives and honorable things about them. Many of us have trained ourselves to scan people's lives until we see what isn't perfect or doesn't measure up, and we focus completely there. That will turn you into a cynic and a critic, and your words will carry anger and bitterness with them regularly.

1 6. Your anger temperament says that it all depends on you to succeed.

> "Come now, you who say, 'Today or tomorrow we will go to such and such a city, and spend a year there and engage in business and make a profit.'"
>
> **(James 4:13)**

a. How much do you attribute your own success to your own efforts?

b. Are you open to involving God in your dreams, goals, and plans? Do you see value in that?

If you are an energetic person, it is easy to believe or think that it is all up to you to achieve your goals. Your anger will fuel your hard work, but it will often be at the expense of your relationships. Jesus asks, "What does it profit a man if he gains the whole world but loses his soul?" If you don't have a relationship with God and others, what good is your work, striving, and possessions?

We should make plans and submit them to the Lord in prayer. We should be willing to involve God in developing our dreams, goals, and plans and be open to His revisions and changes. Goals and plans energize leaders and action-oriented people, so keep them connected to God and subject to His redirections.

17. You do not control the future; you just think you do.

"Yet you do not know what your life will be like tomorrow. You are just a vapor that appears for a little while and then vanishes away. Instead, you ought to say, 'If the Lord wills, we will live and also do this or that.'"
(James 4:14–15)

a. Are you a person who tends to plan everything about their future? What happens to your emotions when things don't work out?

b. How important are your relationships to you?

The future is a wonderful place if we get there with God and great relationships. Get on the same page with God about what is really important. Matthew 22:37–39 tells us that life is all about relationships.

We have the ability to control what we think, what we say, what we do, what emotions we focus on, and our motives. There are little thrusters that we are responsible for which can change quite a bit about our future over time. But we don't control the weather, politics, the economy, and many other things. A little humility in the face of God is wise. We only have the ability to change a small percentage of the future, and even that is if God allows it.

18. **Your arrogant boasting about your ability and predictions of the future come from your temperament and not from a godly place.**

> "But as it is, you boast in your arrogance; all such boasting is evil."
>
> **(James 4:16)**

a. What role does arrogance play in your future plans and life?

b. Have you ever experienced humiliation when things don't go as planned?

Thinking, acting, or speaking like you completely control your destiny is naïve. Yes, we should make plans, but we should realize that even if we do everything right, it may not happen. Proverbs 21:31 says, "The horse is prepared for battle, but the victory belongs to the Lord."

Your anger and arrogance will increase the likelihood that the outcome you want will not take place.

19. **You must live in dependence upon God and realize that many variables are outside your control.**

> "So for one who knows the right thing to do and does not do it, to him it is sin."
>
> **(James 4:17)**

a. What is the right thing to do in the present situation? Can you do that even though it is hard?

b. How does God want you to use the refined energy from your anger and the wisdom from His Spirit to accomplish something right?

c. Give some thought to the sins of omission you may commit without meaning to. They occur far more often than the intentional sins of commission and wickedness.

Dear Heavenly Father,

I come in the Name of the Lord Jesus Christ and ask You to show me what I should do and what I should say. I realize that, in many cases, I have ignored Your prompting and Your wisdom, but I now want to take full advantage of Your relationship with me. I want to be directed by Your guidance and not just my own. I want to downregulate my anger and do the right thing. I want to empower others and not just myself. I need Your power to do the right things. I no longer want to live my life dependent on my anger or be the slave of my anger. I want a new life full of great relationships because I have proven I can control my anger.

Amen

ANGER RESET NEXT STEPS

You have finished all twenty-seven days of the anger reset process. You are now aware of all kinds of strategies, techniques, prayers, and exercises that will allow you to escape from the slavery of anger. However, it will take more than just reading this book to bring about change. You might need to try each of the exercises multiple times to see which ones help you get a handle on your anger. Not every strategy will work for you. Some will and some won't.

I hope you will work through this material a second and third time as an exercise manual and find seven to ten exercises that consistently allow you to contain, control, or calm your anger. Write your strategies on a card you carry with you. Put the seven to ten that work on your phone so you can refer to them when needed. Memorize the verses for those exercises and techniques so that the Bible is working in your soul. Regularly speak biblical verses about remaining calm and not expressing rage and anger under your breath. Meditating on the Bible in these ways will help tremendously. You can become someone who has control over your spirit; someone people can trust to lead them and remain calm when things don't go your way. Step into the person you were meant to be, following the prompting of God to make changes to yourself and your situation. It has been a pleasure serving you through the pages of this book. As the first in the Spiritual Warfare Series, look for the rest of the books to continue the fight. I pray these exercises help you become the person you are meant to be and that your relationships flourish because of your hard work.

In Him,

Dr. Gil Stieglitz

WHAT ANGER RESET STRATEGIES WILL I TRY?

1. _____

2. _____

3. _____

4. _____

5. _____

6. _____

7. _____

8. _____

9. _____

10. _____

NOTES

[1] Marvel Comics, *The Incredible Hulk,* Copyright ©1962.

[2] Viktor E. Frankl, *Man's Search for Meaning* (Boston, MA: Beacon Press, 2006).

[3] Google, "What is meant by lizard brain," accessed August 2, 2024.

[4] "What is anger management?" WebMD.com, medically reviewed by Jennifer Casarella, MD, on August 28, 2022, https://www.webmd.com/mental-health/anger-management.

[5] Kevin A. Thompson, *Stay in Your Lane: Worry Less, Love More, and Get Things Done* (Roseville, CA: Thrive Media, 2023).

[6] Stephen R. Covey, *The 7 Habits of Highly Effective Families: Creating a Nurturing Family in a Turbulent World* (New York City: St. Martin's Publishing Group, 2022).

[7] "When I was a son to my father, Tender and the only son in the sight of my mother, Then he taught me and said to me, 'Let your heart hold fast my words; Keep my commandments and live; Acquire wisdom! Acquire understanding! Do not forget nor turn away from the words of my mouth'" (Proverbs 4:3–6).

[8] "Binah," Bible Hub, https://biblehub.com/hebrew/998.htm.

[9] "Da'at," Blue Letter Bible, https://www.blueletterbible.org/lexicon/h1847/kjv/wlc/0-1/.

[10] Joseph Grenny, Kerry Patterson, et al. *Crucial Conversations*, Third Edition (New York: McGraw Hill Publishing, 2022), 77–80.

[11] Joe Polish, *What's in It for Them?* (Carlsbad, CA: Hay House Publishing, 2022).

[12] Paul Johnson, *Intellectuals: From Marx to Tolstoy to Sartre and Chomsky* (New York: Harper Perennial, 2007).

[13] James Leath, "A Story of Anger and Forgiveness: Nails in the Fence," May 8, https://www.jamesleath.com/notes/a-story-of-anger-and-forgiveness.

14 Gerald Schroder, *The Hidden Face of God: Science Reveals the Ultimate Truth* (New York City: Touchstone of Simon and Schuster, 2001), 92–104.

15 Gil Stieglitz, *They Laughed When I Wrote Another Book on Prayer: How to Make Prayer Work* (Roseville, CA: PTLB Publishing, 2011).

16 Ron Howard, et al., *Apollo 13*, Universal, 2005.

17 Jack Nicklaus, *Golf My Way* (New York City: Simon and Schuster, 2005).

18 Lea Winerman, "The Mind's Mirror," American Psychological Association, apa.org, October 2005, Vol 36, No. 9, print version: pg. 48, https://www.apa.org/monitor/oct05/mirror.

19 James Martin, S.J., *The Jesuit Guide to (Almost) Everything: A Spirituality for Real Life* (New York City: HarperOne, 2010).

20 Louise Pistole, "When Will the Waves Stop: Can Anxiety and Gratitude Coexist in our Minds?" https://www.louisepistole.com/when-will-the-waves-stop-can-anxiety-and-gratitude-coexist-in-our-minds/.

21 Tony Robbins, "Who Is in Charge of Your Emotions?" Thrive Global, October 27, 2017, https://medium.com/thrive-global/who-is-in-charge-of-your-emotions-e533396a7806.

22 Dan Sullivan, Dr. Benjamin Hardy, et al., *The Gap and the Gain* (Carlsbad, CA: Hay House Publsihing, 2021).

23 "Shalom," Biblehub.org, https://biblehub.com/hebrew/7965.htm.

24 Dan J. Siegel, M.D., *Personality and Wholeness in Therapy* (New York City: W.W. Norton & Company, Inc., 2024), 43f.

25 Daniel Lappin, *Thou Shall Prosper: Ten Commandments for Making Money* (Hoboken, NJ: John Wiley & Sons, Inc., 2010).

ABOUT THE AUTHOR

Dr. Gil Stieglitz is a prolific author, engaging speaker, and insightful pastor who has written over thirty books on marriage, parenting, soul development, and spiritual warfare. *The Anger Reset: 27 Days to a Calmer You* is the first book in his Spiritual Warfare Series. Other books on spiritual warfare include *The Schemes of Satan, Satan and the Origin of Evil, Why There Has to Be a Hell, Breaking Satanic Bondage,* and *Weapons of Righteousness.*

Gil speaks to thousands of people each year about the wonders of God's wisdom and principles. He currently serves as a discipleship pastor at Bayside Church, a dynamic multi-site church near Sacramento, CA. He founded Principles To Live By (PTLB), a nonprofit organization that helps people connect to God's principles in everyday life. He and his wife, Dana, reside in Northern California and have three adult daughters. For more information about his books and speaking, visit www.ptlb.com.

OTHER PTLB PUBLISHING RESOURCES

Spiritual Warfare and Personal Transformation

Breaking Spiritual Bondage by **Dr. Gil Stieglitz**

Spiritual Disciplines of a C.H.R.I.S.T.I.A.N. by **Gil Stieglitz**

Becoming Courageous by **Gil Stieglitz**

The Keys to Grapeness by **Gil Stieglitz**

Deep Happiness by **Gil Stieglitz**

Secrets of God's Armor by **Gil Stieglitz**

The Schemes of Satan by **Gil Stieglitz**

Satan and the Origin of Evil by **Gil Stieglitz**

Why There Has to Be a Hell by **Gil Stieglitz**

The Gift of Seeing Angels and Demons by **Dr. Susan Merritt**

Weapons of Righteousness by **Gil Stieglitz**

Uniquely You Workbook by **Jenny T. Williamson**

For more additional resources and to learn about the mission and purpose of Principles to Live By, visit PTLB.com. Books are available at Amazon.com, Barnes&Noble.com, and Target.com.

Made in the USA
Columbia, SC
03 April 2025

56101287R00124